Artistry on Ice

Figure Skating Skills and Style

Nancy Kerrigan
with Mary Spencer

D0731297

Human Kinetics

Library of Congress Cataloging-in-Publication Data

Kerrigan, Nancy, 1969-
   Artistry on ice / Nancy Kerrigan with Mary Spencer.
     p. cm.
   ISBN 0-7360-3697-0 (soft cover)
    1. Skating. I. Spencer, Mary, 1975-   II. Title.
   GV850.4 .K47   2003
   796.91—dc21   2002010631

ISBN: 0-7360-3697-0

Developmental Editor: Leigh LaHood; **Copyeditor:** Jacqueline Eaton Blakley; **Proofreader:** Sarah Wiseman; **Graphic Designer:** Nancy Rasmus; **Graphic Artist:** Sandra Meier; **Photo Managers:** Leslie A. Woodrum and Dan Wendt; **Cover Designer:** Keith Blomberg; **Photographer (cover):** Tom Roberts; **Photographer (interior):** Photo on page 33 © Sport the Library/Robb Cox; photo on page 113 © SportsChrome USA; photo on page 195 © Bongarts/SportsChrome USA; all other photos by Tom Roberts, except where noted otherwise; **Art Manager:** Carl D. Johnson; **Illustrator:** Mic Greenberg; **Printer:** Butler & Tanner Ltd.

Human Kinetics books are available at special discounts for bulk purchase. Special editions or book excerpts can also be created to specification. For details, contact the Special Sales Manager at Human Kinetics.

Printed in England

10 9 8 7 6 5 4 3 2 1

Human Kinetics
Web site: www.HumanKinetics.com

United States: Human Kinetics
P.O. Box 5076
Champaign, IL 61825-5076
800-747-4457
e-mail: humank@hkusa.com

Canada: Human Kinetics
475 Devonshire Road Unit 100
Windsor, ON N8Y 2L5
800-465-7301 (in Canada only)
e-mail: orders@hkcanada.com

Europe: Human Kinetics
107 Bradford Road
Stanningley
Leeds LS28 6AT, United Kingdom
+44 (0) 113 255 5665
e-mail: hk@hkeurope.com

Australia: Human Kinetics
57A Price Avenue
Lower Mitcham, South Australia 5062
08 8277 1555
e-mail: liahka@senet.com.au

New Zealand: Human Kinetics
P.O. Box 105-231, Auckland Central
09-523-3462
e-mail: hkp@ihug.co.nz

Artistry on Ice

Figure Skating
Skills and Style

Contents

Acknowledgments   vi
Introduction   vii

Part I   Preparing to Skate   1

1   Essential Skills   5
2   Spirals   15
3   Spread Eagles and Ina Bauers   23
4   Lunges   29

Part II   Mastering Spins   33

5   Scratch Spins   37
6   Sit Spins   43
7   Camel Spins   49
8   Spin Variations   57

Part III	Nailing Jumps		65
	9	Salchows	71
	10	Toe Loops	77
	11	Loops	81
	12	Flips	87
	13	Lutzes	91
	14	Axels	97
	15	Jump Combinations and Variations	105
Part IV	Skating With a Partner		113
	16	Ice Dancing	119
	17	Pairs Skating	129
	18	Basic Lifts	139
	19	Synchronized Skating	151
Part V	Training Off the Ice		159
	20	Off-Ice Training Concepts	163
	21	Warming Up and Cooling Down	169
	22	Land and Water Exercises	177
Part VI	Preparing for Competition		195
	23	Music	199
	24	Choreography	205
	25	Costumes	213
	26	The Total Package	221
Summary			227
References and Suggested Reading			229
About the Authors			231

Acknowledgments

Just as any solid skating program involves employing experts, we have asked a few noted coaches to serve as consultants in the writing of this book. These include renowned land and water therapy expert and founder of the Burdenko Land and Water Therapy Institute, Igor Burdenko; noted exercise physiologist and personal trainer, Jessica Regnante; national pairs champion and 1980 Olympian, Sheryl Franks; pairs coach and former principal with Holiday on Ice, Bobby Martin; internationally renowned synchronized skating coach of the Haydennettes and Ice Mates, Lynn Benson; and international dance competitor and ice dancing professional and choreographer, Collin Sullivan. Each expert contributed their knowledge to assist the authors. Additionally, the authors wish to thank internationally renowned ice dance coach, Barret Brown; former international competitor, current professional skater and writer, Ron Kravette, and international competitor and professional ballroom dancer, Mark Nocera, for their insights and review of specific chapters of the book.

In addition to the skating experts, the authors also wish to thank and acknowledge the work of Ted Miller and Leigh LaHood of Human Kinetics. Without their patience, perseverance, and support, the project would not have become a reality. We also thank Tom Roberts for making the long trip to a cold ice rink to shoot such beautiful pictures. Thanks also go to the Stoneham Ice Arena and the Lexington Club for providing space to shoot the photos and all of the models for their time, positive energy, and great technique.

Both authors also thank their coaches and supporters for their inspiration, instruction, and support. Specific thanks go to Jerry Solomon for his vision, support, and implementation of this project, as well as his belief and love. Finally, sincere thanks and appreciation to our families and friends. Thank you to those who assisted in the writing, reading, and review of each chapter and to all for your support, guidance, and friendship. Without you, this project would only exist in our hearts and minds.

Introduction

I am very pleased to present *Artistry on Ice!* This book gives me the opportunity to share many of the tips that have helped me find joy and success on the ice. I began skating at the age of six and continued to do so because I loved to go fast and perform. Skating has allowed me to express myself in a sport that combines athleticism, musicality, theatrics, and dance.

Unlike other books on skating, *Artistry on Ice* is not focused on the early fundamentals. This book is intended for intermediate to advanced skaters of all ages and includes tips for those who want to sharpen their competitive skills. By following clear, easy instructions and viewing the photographs that accompany them, you will perfect the skills you need to advance to higher levels of learning. In each chapter you will learn several techniques for each move. As you read the book and try out these skills, keep in mind that some tips and techniques will work better for you than others. There is no "right way" to achieve success. Working with your coach, you can find variations that work better for you and your body. However, just as with sewing or cooking, you need to know the rules before you can break or change them.

Although I will offer many tips, I advise you to focus on one thing as you learn to perfect skills. My tendency in the past was to think about too many things while trying to learn and execute skills, especially when learning jumps. For my double Axel, I used to think about my arms passing by my sides moving along my body and back, but keeping my elbows straight, not bent, and then coming through, but not higher than my shoulders. Then I had to think of passing the free leg through close, moving it beyond the skating leg with a bent knee, and so on. I eventually realized that I didn't have enough time for all of these thoughts. Instead, I learned to pick one cue that would trigger the proper technique and cause me to land the jump easily. As you read each chapter, keep this in mind. I can tell you what worked for me, but only you and your coach can determine what is right for you.

Learning to become a better skater is a challenging process, but it is rewarding to find out what you are capable of. As I've faced difficulties in perfecting new moves, I've often found that breaking down problems to a more basic level has helped me to solve them. Although good coaches are part of the success equation, skaters must also examine and fix errors themselves. When I first began to take lessons with my coach, Evy Scotvold, he made me do single jumps for a month. It was a difficult process, and for a while it hurt my pride. I was already working on triples by then, and I thought, *What is he doing? Why is he making me do this?* Now I know that he was teaching me the technique for all of my jumps, because if I can do a single I can almost always figure out what is going wrong with the double or triple. Even now, if I'm having problems and I can't figure out why a particular jump is not working, I'll return to singles or something more basic. In this book, you too will find that the fundamentals lay the groundwork for advanced moves, so it is very important to not only work hard but also to work correctly.

Artistry on Ice is broken into easy-to-read segments that build on the skills from each part to the final chapter. We begin with part 1, "Preparing to Skate." This section begins with some of the essential skills that all skaters need to know to advance in the sport. From there, specific moves that are found in choreography, or Moves in the Field, are presented. Then we will spin into part 2, covering the basic spins and a few fun variations. From there we will jump into part 3, covering the basic jumps and their variations.

In the second half of the book, I have consulted a few experts to add their thoughts and insights. If you enjoy skating with one partner or many, you can't miss part 4, in which we cover ice dance, pairs, and synchronized skating. In part 5, we will step off the ice to discuss some of the training tips that have helped me and that I hope will help you to succeed on the ice. Finally, in part 6, we will put all of the skills that you have learned together to prepare you for competition. This will cover music, costumes, choreography, and my personal competition insights.

Through photography, easy-to-follow tips, and personal anecdotes, I'll share with you the techniques I have learned throughout my career and the skills that have helped me to succeed. I hope that you will enjoy reading it and have fun with your skating. Remember that although it may look as if I know what I'm doing now, it wasn't always that way. If you work hard, work intelligently, and have faith in yourself, you will have fun and success!

Part 1

Preparing to Skate

My coaches have always stressed that it is important to be a good all-around skater. Being a good skater is not just about being able to jump high or spin fast—it's also about skating with speed, deep edges, and interesting choreography in a way that impresses the audience and judges with technique and artistry. In the coming chapters we discuss several skating moves that all skaters should learn, including turns, spirals, spread eagles, Ina Bauers, and lunges. Although I did not specifically study Moves in the Field, I will give you some tips on basic skating technique that may be applied to those tests and to your general skating. Remember, all of these skills are not only good to learn to create exciting and interesting programs, they are also fun!

Every skater knows that part of learning to skate is having a great teacher. Advanced skaters need someone who knows their strengths and weaknesses and is able to draw the best out of them. Although you may already have found a great instructor, that does not guarantee a successful coach–student relationship. Success requires a solid coach, a good skater who is willing to learn, and a strong base of support from parents or guardians. The coach and student must respect each other and be able to work well together. Before we begin skating, let's briefly discuss the important qualities a good instructor should have and the skills that good skaters should know.

The Coach

Whether you work with a *coach* or an *instructor* depends on how seriously you want to train. There is a difference between an instructor and a coach. An instructor teaches you about skating but does not help to direct your career and make decisions about your training in the same ways that a coach does. If you are choosing a coach for the first time, make sure that you and the coach are compatible. You will need to meet with him and (if possible) talk to his students to get a feel for his personality and teaching style.

It is important that family members be compatible with the coach as well. Your family should not coach you, but they do need to be able to support and respect your coach. You also need to know whether your coach has a training system in place and has established relationships with other trainers as well as how she interacts with other instructors. Finally, you need to understand her time commitments and how she handles competitions. Be sure to discuss how many lessons you expect to have and how she charges for her time.

If you are choosing a coach for what you hope will be a long-term relationship, you need to keep in mind some additional considerations. Many skaters choose a coach based on reputation. This often works well because a coach's reputation is established by the performance of his or her students. However, just as some excellent doctors are very skilled in their work but aren't able to teach others the fundamentals in medicine, so too some excellent skaters can't teach others to skate. Skating is a beautiful sport—it combines artistry, emotion, and dance—but it is also very technical. You need a coach who understands the technique and is able to communicate it clearly and effectively so that you progress.

Every skater is different. We all have different bodies and different ways of learning. Some people are visual learners who can see a move and copy it. Others need to feel the move or have someone place them in the proper position to feel the correct technique. Still others need to have a move thoroughly explained before they attempt it. Some professionals teach without actually working on the ice with their students. This can be difficult for a visual learner, who should look for a coach who is on the ice often with students. It is important that a coach tailor her methods to your body and your learning style so that you will learn as efficiently as possible.

A good coach should have your best interests in mind and work with you to achieve your goals. I didn't want to move away from home, so I looked for good instructors in my area. Not everyone who wants to seriously pursue skating will be able to find the kind of coach he or she needs nearby—many rinks don't have enough instructors. In the same way, a pairs skater or ice dancer looking for a partner might have to move away from home. Your coach needs to let you go, if that is necessary, or work with you to find a suitable training environment in your area.

In baseball, coaches for different positions and skills work together to help the team succeed. Skating also has specialists who are skilled in different aspects of the sport. Some coaches don't allow their students to work with other coaches. Your coach should be willing to encourage your growth so that you will be able to reach your goals. My coaches, Evy and Mary Scotvold, occasionally asked me to accompany them to competitions as a substitute if one or the other couldn't attend. In trying to help coach, I would tell skaters the same thing that Evy and Mary had told them a million times before, then watch as the skaters correctly completed the technique. Sometimes the same lesson can be taught slightly differently, or because it is coming from someone else, it suddenly becomes clear.

Pairs and ice dancers especially should work with more than one instructor and should seek out the help of both a man and a woman. A man will best be able to explain to another man how to do a lift, whereas a woman is usually best able to explain to another woman how to be lifted. This rule has exceptions, but generally a man and a woman should at least be available to act as consultants in these cases.

The following are some other questions to consider:

- Is the coach accredited? The Professional Skaters' Association (PSA) offers a variety of testing and training programs to help coaches gain teaching credentials.
- Has he or she continued to learn about her sport? Skating is constantly evolving. A good coach will evolve with it by keeping up with trends, reading trade publications, working with other pros, and knowing the

rules of the U.S. Figure Skating Association (USFSA). A good coach knows that there is always more to learn.

The Student

A coach is a strong motivator, but she cannot make students skate. As a student, *you* must have a strong desire to learn and be determined to work. Skating is not always as easy as it looks. To learn, you must persevere through the difficult times when a move is not coming quickly and practice until it does happen. This includes practicing alone, without a coach's supervision, to work on techniques from lessons. Practice time allows you to make discoveries on your own and to think about what you have learned in the lesson. At a competition, your coach isn't on the ice with you saying, "OK, now do it again because you didn't bring your arms through all the way." You need to know the technique to fix problems by yourself.

Students must accept change and be open to the coach's advice. Sometimes a coach is trying to get you to do something because he sees potential. I don't think any coach intentionally tries to hurt students' feelings, but a coach may occasionally try to frustrate a student if other attempts at teaching aren't working. Try to understand that a coach's criticism is not meant to personally injure you, but to help you become a better skater.

If you have questions, ask. A good student is always trying to learn more, so if you don't understand why your coach is making you do something, ask why. The coach may be able to rephrase or further explain if there has been a misunderstanding.

You may have days when, no matter how hard you try, you are just frustrating yourself and hammering in a bad habit. Pride says, "I will fix it!" Because sessions are often paid for, and because you don't want to give up, it can be hard to get off the ice and go home—and sometimes you *are* able to fix the problem by staying and working through it. However, there are also times when the smartest thing to do is to say, "I'll fix it tomorrow." Skating is all about timing and being loose and relaxed. The more frustrated you become, the harder it is to control your body and your muscles tighten. So it is occasionally best to move on or leave it for the next day. Following are some general tips that should help you as a skating student:

- Carry a notebook to your lessons so that you and your coach can write down key points from the day's instruction.
- After lessons, spend a few moments practicing and reviewing the key points in order to remember the changes in your body.
- Show up to lessons on time and be prepared. It is the best way to get the most out of the process.

Above all, try your best, respect your coaches, and work hard. We all have bad days from time to time, but if you try to keep the skating rink as a place of fun and learning, the bad days will not seem so bad. Now, let's start skating!

1

Essential Skills

In skating today, a great deal of emphasis is placed on jumping, spinning, and big tricks. Singles skaters and pairs are supposed to skate faster and do more elements to be noticed in competition. Ice dancers and synchronized skaters, too, have been pushed athletically to achieve more. Sports are about who can do the most, and do it best. However, skating is more than jumping, spinning, and lifting. Watching a truly gifted artistic skater like Paul Wylie or Brian Boitano removes all doubt that it is not only what they do with their bodies in the air that makes them great but also the patterns they leave behind on the ice.

When I was training as an amateur, I spent hours every day tracing my figures. In 1990, figures were removed from the International Skating Union (ISU) competition structure. Although I understand why figures were omitted from the sport, I miss the knowledge of strong basic skating they provided. As I have skated in, choreographed, and produced shows as a professional skater, I have seen that skaters with strong fundamentals not only have longer careers but are also more enjoyable to watch.

Moves in the Field have replaced figures in the test structure, but I'm not sure these are giving skaters what they really need. Many seem to take 10 minutes out of a freeskate session to run through them and then move on to the rest of the session. The quality of what is intended does not seem to be there.

Speed, posture, knee bend, and edge control are very important to create a strong overall presentation. These things can be taught in Moves in the Field, but they must also be practiced in all aspects of your skating. In this chapter I will discuss a few of these basic principles. Although I didn't have to take the Moves in the Field tests, many of the skills that I have learned over the years and through my figure training have taught me how to be a better skater—I hope they will help you too!

Power Sessions

Power sessions helped my training and development immeasurably. Many clubs and rinks still run these sessions. At the training center I skated at, the sessions were run by Evy, and they were very hard! He made us skate fast while performing difficult footwork sections and basic skating moves. It also gave us an opportunity to do things off the ice. I actually learned butterflies and some of my jump technique off the ice in a group power class. As Paul Wylie and I got older and higher in the ranks, Evy would say, "I'm not coming in today. You're going to teach power. Let me know how they do, and don't go easy." The sessions gave Paul and me a chance to try out teaching. When you are teaching, you have to think about what the truly important aspects of a skill are and figure out how to communicate that to others in a way they can understand.

Many ice theater groups and ice shows run weekly classes. In these classes, skaters are often taught to practice moves in both directions and on both feet, similar to Moves in the Field. If you are in a show (or even if you are a competitor) you may do the same program over and over again for a year or two. When you are working on the program, you tend to center your warm-up and earlier sessions on skills needed for your program. For example, you may warm up only with jump combinations that you do in your program. However, when you decide it's time for a new program, you'll struggle with it initially because you haven't practiced all of your other skills. It is good to continue to work on all of your skating moves, either in classes or on your own, so that you will keep all of your skills sharp and fresh and you don't have to relearn them.

Posture

Good posture is necessary in all skating disciplines. Just as in figures, skaters need to stand upright with the chest and head lifted and the abdominal muscles controlled (figure 1.1). The number-one error I see skaters make in the Moves and even in their general skating is holding the arms too high, almost at shoulder height. If your arms are high, you don't have control of your body, and your skating looks awkward. It is a lot easier to control your body, your center of gravity, and your weight transfer if your arms are waist

a   b

Figure 1.1   Good posture is essential for all movements, including *(a)* forward crossovers and *(b)* back crossovers.

high or even hip high. You should feel as if you are pushing down with the palm or the heel of your hand on a table so that you have control.

Correct arm posture will also give you a little bit of tension in your muscles. (You don't want to feel tension in your whole body because you want some flexibility and space to move.) If your arms are up, you don't have the muscle tension you need to control quick movements from edge to edge. The same applies to jumps—without control of your arm movements, you won't land them. So work on keeping those arms down with your back muscles pulling down into your waist so that you are best able to control your upper body.

Speed

In Moves in the Field and in general skating, speed is a necessity. Speed comes from lifting out of the knee and pushing off the whole blade. When you skate, your knees should be very active. They do not stay in a static up or down position; you want to be able to use them to gain power and speed.

A good push should use your whole blade to increase your flow across the ice. Push off your whole foot, pushing down through the ankle and through the toe, using the ice to push off. That's why speed skaters have such long blades—the length gives them more to stroke off and through to increase their flow with less effort. With the speed you get from a good push, you will be able to cover the ice surface more completely. You may eventually find that what may have once taken four strokes now takes only one or two.

Using the Whole Ice Surface

A lot of people are taught jumps and spins and many other basic skating techniques and moves, but they are not taught to use the ice. Toller Cranston, the 1976 Olympic bronze medalist, once came up to me at a competition and said, "Nancy, you were the only one who used the ice. The corners. You were in the corners. You went fast and you used the whole surface." It was such a compliment that I remember it to this day. People forget in choreography and in their general skating to use the whole ice surface. Now that I skate in shows, I realize how much harder it is. I go from a small surface to a big surface quite often and I am always surprised by how much harder I have to push to cover the ice.

Edges and Lobes

Ice dancers know that every edge is skated on a lobe. A lobe is a half circle. To position your blade on a true edge, you must draw complete lobes (figure 1.2). Thus, to practice a right outside edge, you begin by stroking directly into the center of the ice and finish by stroking directly into the boards. To accurately place your feet, you must work to have neat feet, keeping your steps close to each other. A wide step generally leaves a lot of room for the skater to misstep or set an incomplete edge.

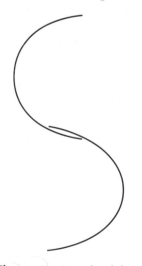

Having deep edges on your blades does help you to skate on deep edges with full lobes. People are sometimes afraid to have a deep edge on their skates, but it can be a big help. I was doing a show once, and the skate sharpener asked me, "Are you sure this is how you have your skates sharpened? Singles skaters don't usually have their blades this sharp." I said, "Well, I do." If I am sideways landing a jump, with a deep edge I have a better chance of being able to save it.

Many skaters don't have deep edges, but they worry about nicks in their blades. A nick just slows you down—it doesn't ruin your skating. It is only if you lose an edge that you really can't do anything, because you just slide right off. So having

Figure 1.2   Complete lobes.

nicks means that you need to push harder and use

the ice more. That isn't necessarily a bad thing for skating, and when the edges are sharp you will generally find that your flow is greatly improved.

Edge Quality

One of the things that separate skaters from one another is edge quality. You can't have edge quality without power, and power comes from knee bend. Dorothy Hamill, for example, has beautiful knees. She can skate cleanly with solid flow and beautiful extension in footwork or edges in sequence. She has been skating for years, and there is a quality to her movement that

© J. Barry Mittan

One of figure skating's greats, Dorothy Hamill is known for clean, deep edges and graceful movements.

is wonderful to watch. Knee bend also allows you to rock easily and quickly from edge to edge so that you skate on deep lobes.

A move that is good for working on knees and edgework is the forward and backward power change of edge pulls, something I had to do in power sessions. The USFSA Rulebook says that the primary focus of this move is power. In power pulls you have to use your knee to change and pull the edge quickly—you want to pull up and out of the edge and then get quickly back down into your knee (figure 1.3). It is hard work on the thighs, but, if done correctly, this move will teach you speed, edge control, rhythm, and lobing. Don't forget about your posture and upper-body control. The less work you create for yourself above, the more you will be able to focus on your knee bend.

Rhythm

In all of your Moves in the Field, you want to set a steady rhythm. A Move that specifies quickness doesn't require that you rush through; it requires that you set an even rhythm that is fast. I talked Evy into letting us listen to

a   b

Figure 1.3   Power pulls, changing from *(a)* inside to *(b)* outside edges. Notice the zigzag pattern on the ice.

music on our figure sessions. I found that it not only relaxed me, but it also helped me to set a rhythm to the pushes and turns. Cat Stevens and James Taylor songs were good for keeping me calm and consistent. The important thing to keep in mind in the Moves in the Field or in any footwork is that you don't want to skate fast on one part and then slow down on the part that's harder for you. Set an even tempo with an even rhythm to your knee bend and pushes so that even on your difficult sequences you maintain consistent flow.

Turns

Another important aspect of Moves in the Field and skating in general is turning. I am a little concerned, with the loss of figures, that skaters don't understand the vocabulary of skating, so I'll explain a few basic turns here.

THREE TURN. A *three turn* is a one-foot turn that can be started forward or backward on either edge. The edge you start on is different from the edge you finish on and will stay on the same lobe. For example, a forward outside three finishes on a back inside edge. The turn looks like the number 3 on the ice (figure 1.4a).

MOHAWK. A *mohawk* is a two-foot turn that can be started forward or backward on either edge. The edge you start on is the same as the edge you finish on and will stay on the same lobe. For example, a forward inside mohawk finishes on a back inside edge (figure 1.4b and c).

CHOCTAW. A *choctaw* is a two-foot turn that can be executed starting forward or backward on either edge. The edge you start on is different from the edge you finish on and will take you on a new lobe. For example, in a closed choctaw you could start on a forward inside edge and finish on a backward outside edge (figure 1.4d).

BRACKET. A *bracket* is a one-foot turn that can be started forward or backward on either edge. The edge you start on is different from the edge you finish on, but you stay on the same lobe. For example, you could start on a back inside and turn to a forward outside. It looks like an inverted 3 with the point outward from the lobes (figure 1.4e).

ROCKER. A *rocker* is a one-foot turn that can be started in either direction on either edge. The edge you start on is the same as the edge you finish on with different lobes. For example, you could do a forward outside rocker and turn onto a back outside edge. The center of the turn points inward (figure 1.4f).

COUNTER. A *counter* is a one-foot turn that can be started in either direction on either lobe. The edge you start on is the same as the edge you finish on with different lobes. For example, you could do a forward inside counter and turn onto a back inside edge. The difference between a rocker

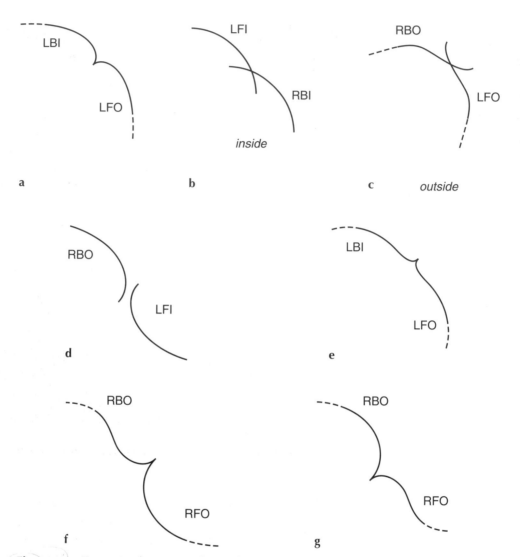

Figure 1.4 Turns: *(a)* three turn, *(b)* inside mohawk, *(c)* outside mohawk, *(d)* choctaw, *(e)* bracket, *(f)* rocker, and *(g)* counter.

and a counter is that in a counter the body rotates opposite the direction of the skating foot, causing the turn to be pointed outward (figure 1.4g).

You will probably learn a variety of ways to execute these turns. I recommend that you start with something simple. On a three turn, it may be easiest to start with your arm and hand out, so it feels as if they are pressing on a table. If you're standing on your left foot for a left outside three turn, your arms will be about waist high with the right hand in front and the left directly behind (figure 1.5a). Move the arms in the direction you want the movement to go (inside the circle, as in figure 1.5b), and then counterrotate for a checkout of the turn to stop rotation for control (figure 1.6).

a   b

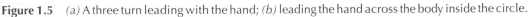

Figure 1.5   *(a)* A three turn leading with the hand; *(b)* leading the hand across the body inside the circle.

In turns you must remember that you need to ride the edge into the turn to let it happen. If you try to force it too quickly, you will probably not have a very good turn. If you are in the proper position, you can turn anywhere. However, you also need to be in a position to be on the circle and ride the edge into the turn.

You also have to be able to check your turns, checking against the rotation before the turn to control the exit. You really don't move much of your upper body at all. It moves a little to keep your balance, but the main movement is in your lower body. Your chest and your center of gravity should be fairly firm.

Increasing Your Performance Diversity

Sometimes when I worked on figures I would draw them on graph paper. I also used to draw out my programs on paper. Seeing a visual breakdown

Figure 1.6 Checking the turn.

of what I was trying to do and comparing it with the rulebook and with my coach's feedback helped me understand how it should look. Some coaches also draw the patterns on the ice.

Moves, just like figures, have a certain pattern they are supposed to follow. When I watch some of the skaters do them, their speed decreases and their lobes get smaller and smaller. Work from the beginning to get your patterns correct, skated on good, solid lobes, then move on and work from there. Sometimes you have to break skills down edge by edge to get them right. Once you master them, you are more likely to maintain them because you understand them thoroughly.

Good technique in Moves in the Field and general skating should positively influence your skating as a whole. Some people don't take the Moves seriously, thinking, "Oh, I'll just get through these and get the tests done." If you want to skate your best, you must master these basic skills.

Skating keeps changing and evolving. As it changes, I hope that there will be more opportunities for more skaters, not just the elite athletes. For example, being able to spin both directions or do spread eagles both ways could help to set you apart from other skaters and open doors for you. These days, skaters are able to have more of an "afterlife" when they are finished with their competitive careers. For example, as a show producer, if I'm hiring 10 background line skaters, I want 10 people who can do Ina Bauers both ways for choreography purposes. So keep in mind that these skills may not only help you to be a better skater today, but may also give you a future in professional skating. The ability to skate well with a diverse array of skills not only lengthens your career, but it also gives your skating extra polish.

2

Spirals

The spiral is one of my favorite moves. Simple yet effective, it is much harder to do than it looks—but it should always *look* easy. My favorite variation is the spiral with my hand to my knee. I don't think that this spiral really has a name, though I am always flattered when I hear people call it "Nancy's spiral." I don't remember anyone else doing that spiral before me, and I can't quite remember how I first began doing it. I do know that I have been doing the variation since I was about 14. As I look back through old photo albums, I find many pictures of myself in this spiral, sometimes in very strange costumes!

In this chapter I will explain how to do the four main spirals and will offer a few tips on spiral variations. Perhaps, as you become more comfortable with the spiral, you will find ways to make it one of your signature moves!

Starting Out

Spirals can be done forward or backward, on outside or inside edges. Most of the general concepts are the same: you should have a nice stretch, with your free leg lifted up and out from your waist. According to the USFSA Rulebook, your free leg should be higher than hip level in a spiral sequence, so as long as your knee is lifted to at least that point, you have many options.

In all spirals, you begin by standing at the boards and slowly lifting your free leg as you glide on one foot. Many skaters begin spirals by dropping their upper bodies forward and then lifting their legs, but this is not ideal.

We don't all have ballerina-like stretch, so it is natural for the upper body to release forward a little bit. However, dropping the upper body forward first is not a good idea because it could cause you to go over your toe pick and land on your face! I have a friend who actually hit her teeth doing spirals.

Start slowly and find your balance point in your skate as you gradually lift your leg in the air. At the same time, always remember to pull up and out of your waist with your chest lifted and your neck extended so that you can hold your balance. The end result is that your leg should be lifted to about 90 degrees or higher. Proper technique will create long, elegant lines and will also help the audience see your face and smile.

Remember what your free leg is doing: it should be stretched with a pointed toe. Many people talk about turning out from the hip, but because we all have different bodies, what works for one might not work for another. (I can't turn out from the hip, for example.) Think about turning out from wherever you can—whether it is turning out from the toe, the knee, or the hip—so that the leg is stretched with a pointed toe. It is hard to point your toe in a skate, so I have had my heel cut back in my skate like a dancer's boot. It doesn't affect my jumps and allows me to get the extra stretch and toe point that I want.

Figure 2.1 Looking forward during a spiral helps maintain balance.

Forward Spirals

Just as in riding a bike, look ahead as you begin to release into the forward spiral—this helps to maintain a balance point (figure 2.1). Especially when the body is going forward, skaters tend to look down for fear of losing control. Many times we try to save ourselves by putting our hands out to prevent a fall. This actually increases the chance of falling, as your upper body follows your arms. Instead, look out and forward, not focusing directly down. This will also prevent you from going over your toe pick and from hitting others.

Most important, in a spiral you need to be balanced. As you release into the forward spiral, try to keep your balance at the same point. I actually think of keeping my weight back on the blade; as your upper body goes forward into the spiral, your weight tends to shift forward on the blade as well. By thinking of keeping the weight back, you will keep your weight centered in the middle of the foot. Finding the balance point will make you more comfortable in the spiral, allowing for extra extension and a fuller spiral position.

As you work on the basic forward spiral, your leg will get higher. No matter how high your free leg is, you still want to keep the chest and abdomen lifted so that the audience can see your face and an attractive, confident upper-body position. You should feel that you are lifting up and out of your waist with your shoulders down, not hunched. Often, I think of my arms reaching back to my toe to give me additional stretch in the upper body.

Sasha Cohen maintains a very high spiral while keeping her head lifted and face visible to the audience.

© Rob Tringali, Jr/SportsChrome USA

Above all, remember that if you can't see the audience, they can't see your face. Often, you see skaters with high leg spirals, but you don't see their faces. I don't think it's a nice line, because the skater doesn't look strong from the waist up. It is much more elegant and graceful to have the head up and leg level than to have the leg all the way up in the air. Michelle Kwan, for example, has a very high spiral, but she keeps her head up and turns it slightly so that the audience can see her face. Sasha Cohen and Sarah Hughes also have very high extensions on their spirals but keep their faces visible to the judges and audience. This creates a very effective and attractive spiral position.

Backward Spirals

I'm not a big fan of back spirals because the skater appears to be backing into the audience. However, if they are skated on edges or within a sequence, they can be very effective. A back spiral involves all of the same technique of a forward spiral, except you are now skating backward. It is especially important as you work on back spirals to look backward before you begin. If you are skating your routine in competition, there is no one else on the ice. However, practice sessions are crowded, and it is very easy for another skater to step into your path even when you have the right of way or your music is on. You can't always prevent a collision, but you will have a greater chance if you look behind yourself before you start.

Just as in the forward spiral, think of keeping your upper body lifted. Skating backward, you have an even greater tendency to go forward on your blade. Pull up on your skating toe and back with your shoulders to make sure that you stay near the ball to the middle of the blade. Remember to keep your standing leg's knee straight.

Inside and Outside Spirals

Figure 2.2   Inside spiral.

It took me a long time to figure out how to do inside spirals. I finally discovered that I needed to lift my free hip more and pull my free leg back. When I pull my foot back farther toward the outside of the circle, I skate on an inside edge and the foot becomes my rudder (figure 2.2). Just as with the other spirals, you want to create a long line by keeping your upper body lifted and your free leg extended. You may need to lift your free side higher for an inside spiral, as it is very easy to drop into the circle with the upper body on the inside edge. By thinking of keeping the free side lifted, you will stay up and over the inside edge.

The technique is basically the same for the outside spiral, except your skating foot skates an outside edge (figure 2.3). Your free leg is over the circle, and your free side is slightly back so that your skate is on the outside edge. Just as with the other spirals, lift your head and think of your extension. Although it is considered more difficult to do spirals on edges than on flats, they can be very attractive and effective when done well.

Figure 2.3   Outside spiral.

Spiral Variations

As you begin to feel more comfortable with the spiral, you will no doubt come up with some variations of your own. I think the best way to start doing my favorite spiral is to hold the knee and bring it up to an attitude position before going into the full spiral position. This will help you to feel the balance. The balance point is a little different when you are holding your knee than when you are not. To make a nice line, keep your free leg's knee straight (figure 2.4). This makes it a little harder to hold your knee, but it is worth the extra effort. You may need to dig your nails into your knee and hold on so that it doesn't slip out of position. Also, turning the foot out can create an illusion of a pointed toe, as it is difficult to actually point your toe in an ice skate. This spiral is most effective when it is held for a long time. I often ended my programs with two full circles holding my spiral. This builds the audience's appreciation and applause.

I also like to do a spiral with the knee bent. It is kind of like a high attitude. You can change the movement by reaching for the blade (figure 2.5). Some skaters also use the required spiral sequence to showcase their flexibility.

Figure 2.4 Spiral variation with the hand to the knee.

Sasha Cohen, for example, can lift her leg directly parallel to her ear on her side and hold her knee so that she is in a standing split. Michelle Kwan has brought back the Charlotte spiral, in which she does a back spiral and drops her upper body forward so that her hand touches the ice in front of her. Whatever variations you play with, keep in mind that they should match your music. In some cases, a clean basic spiral that goes with the music is better than an interesting variation that does not.

Men and Spirals

It is not a requirement now, but at one time it was required that men do spirals in their routines. Because it's not required, men don't do them as often now, seemingly thinking that they are too feminine. However, spirals can be done with a very strong, masculine style. Paul Wylie used to do a great spiral. He would start out and go straight down the ice in a stretched spiral directly into a triple flip. It was very difficult and required a great deal

Figure 2.5 Spiral variation, reaching toward the foot.

of strength and flexibility. Many men perhaps don't think that they are flexible enough to do a strong spiral. However, it might be that they should work on their flexibility, since it is such an important part of skating. A flexible muscle is less likely to tear when stretched, thus preventing injury. Like so many skills, flexibility is something to focus on and work to improve. I wouldn't want to see a man do a spiral like I do because I think it would be a little "pretty" for him, but Paul is an excellent example of the strength and stretch a man can have.

Skaters are mainly taught to do moves on one side or in one direction. On moves like spirals, spread eagles, Ina Bauers, and lunges, it's beneficial if you can do the moves on both sides. People are mainly better at moves on their preferred side, but doing things both ways and on both feet offers greater opportunities in footwork, in the spiral sequence, and in choreography, making programs more interesting. A simple, effective spiral can give your skating style!

3

Spread Eagles and Ina Bauers

It took me a long time to learn how to do inside spread eagles; the outside spread eagle was much easier for me. In the beginning, I couldn't hold the extension for very long, and I always seemed to end up back on my heels gliding in a tight circle. Now, after years of practice, and lessons from people like Paul Wylie who do beautiful inside spread eagles, I have learned to do a long inside spread eagle.

For most people, it seems that either the inside or the outside spread eagle is difficult to learn. Our bodies are unique, so it is not uncommon for one to be more natural than the other. However, that doesn't mean we should stop trying. Spread eagles and Ina Bauers are a very effective tool in choreography; they can act as a transition or can be done alone to showcase line and extension. In this chapter I will share some tips on spread eagles and Ina Bauers. Both moves can be started in many ways and offer numerous opportunities for variations. Once you have learned the basic technique, play with them to see what entrances and exits feel most comfortable and how many ways you can vary them.

© J. Barry Mittan

When Paul Wylie executes an inside spread eagle, his body lays out over the edge.

Starting Out

If you are just starting out with spread eagles and Ina Bauers, you may want to begin at the boards to learn the position. Both positions require you to be flexible and loose in the hip muscles, but if they're hard at first don't worry—they can be learned through practice. As you work on them, you may find that one foot is more comfortable in the lead. For me, it was always easiest with my right foot in the lead. I can do it both ways, and you should work to do it with both legs leading, but you may find that one leg is more comfortable than the other in the beginning. Eventually, they will be comfortable in both directions and will be interesting and dynamic moves to put into your choreography.

Outside Spread Eagles

Put your hands on the boards, and with turnout, wedge your feet to the barrier so that they are about shoulder-width apart and in line underneath your hips, as in ballet second position. Remember to keep your belly tucked in—to protect your lower back and for control—and your rear underneath your hips, not sticking out. With your hips still touching the boards, slowly lean back from the waist. Make sure that your legs are straight and your toes are somewhat pointed in your boots. Once this feels comfortable at the barrier, try it gliding.

As you take it out onto the ice, you may want to start with back crossovers. On the last back crossover, flip the front foot forward with the heel leading so that it is placed on the outside edge. You should feel that your hips are pushing forward and your shoulders are pulling back. Just as they were at the boards, your legs should be straight. Feel your chest, upper body, and head lifted (figure 3.1). Your head is the heaviest part of your body—keeping it forward not only ruins the line, but it can also pull you off the edge.

Many skaters complain that they do not have "open hips," so they cannot do spread eagles. I don't have open hips, so for me I don't feel that the position comes from the hips. I think of turning out my ankle and knee and pressing my heels forward. However, for some skaters it is easier to think of the hips.

Although some people naturally have "open hips," you can train your body to become more flexible. Practice stretching on the floor when you are not skating—perhaps when you are watching TV. Try to create the same position while lying face down so that your abdomen, hips, and ankles are flat to the floor. You can also lie on your back with

Figure 3.1 Outside spread eagle.

your knees open to create the same feeling. You have to hold a stretch for 30 seconds to make it really worthwhile. Stretching for 10 seconds is better than not at all, but if you hold something for 30 seconds, then relax, and then hold it again for 30 seconds, it is more beneficial. Remember to breathe while you stretch. Breathing helps to relax your muscles. If you stretch every day, you will decrease your chance of injury and increase elasticity in your muscles. (We will talk more about training in part 5.)

Inside Spread Eagles

You may start working on the inside spread eagle at the boards in the same way—holding the position with your ankles this time rolling slightly to the inside edge. The feeling is the same as the outside spread eagle, with your hips pressing forward, your head up, your shoulders back, and your legs straight, except you are on the inside edge.

When you take it out onto the ice, you can begin in a variety of ways. One way is to start with a forward inside mohawk. The back foot will be on the inside edge first and the front foot will step onto the edge last. The front foot will again guide the edge around. As you begin to feel comfortable with the move, try leaning slightly into the edge. Paul Wylie could do an inside spread eagle and make his body lay out over the edge, just as Brian Boitano can lean in a straight line back on the outside spread eagle. For me, the inside is more comfortable when I stand a little straighter, but always with my hips pressing forward (figure 3.2).

Figure 3.2 Inside spread eagle.

Ina Bauers

Unlike the spread eagle, where both blades are gliding in the same line, in an Ina Bauer one foot is in front of the other. Just as with spread eagles, it is a good idea to practice this move at the boards. Stand with your front foot wedged against the boards and your back foot slightly offset behind it, so that your front heel and your back heel are in the same line. Your front knee should be bent and your back leg should be straight. The hardest part of the Ina is to keep your weight from being too far forward or backward. As you practice at the boards, work to keep your weight equally centered between your feet.

When you take this move out onto the ice, keep the back leg straight and pressing into the ice so that it keeps you stable (figure 3.3). Your front knee should be over your ankle, your weight equally centered on both feet. You may feel a slight stretch in your back thigh as you work to keep the back leg straight. In addition, imagine that someone is pulling your back toe so that it points in your boot (figure 3.4).

Many skaters do a backbend in this move. That was not comfortable for me, so I always tried to make the move dramatic. I liked to start at the end of the rink and skate very fast. Speed, of course, always makes things much more

Figure 3.3 Ina Bauer.

Figure 3.4 The Ina Bauer position should feel like someone is pulling back the toe on the back foot so that it points in the boot.

Figure 3.5 Ina Bauer variation, leaning forward with a graceful arm position.

dynamic and interesting. I would skate down the ice and do the Ina Bauer in a straight line and then slowly transition into a forward lunge that I held to the other end of the rink. It was a simple move, but people always clapped for it.

Whether you do a backbend or stand straight, keep your shoulders down and your back and head up so that the audience can see your face. Another option is to lean forward on the move with a graceful arm position (figure 3.5). Some skaters are able to take this on outside and inside edges, which can also be quite effective.

It seems like we used to see Inas more. Now, all of the jumps have replaced so many of these pretty moves. Keep in mind that they can be done as transitions between moves and can be stylized a number of ways, depending on your program.

Highlighting Your Best Moves

There were always a few moves that just didn't look right on my body, no matter how hard I tried to perfect them. They simply were not my best moves. When you are competing, you have to do required moves, whether they're your best moves or not. In general, though, you want to showcase your best skating in competition or performance. For a year or two, my coaches and I realized that spread eagles didn't fit my body. I couldn't straighten my knees, and the move looked awkward, so we didn't put them in my programs. I continued to practice them throughout that time, and eventually, as I grew and became more limber, we realized that my spread eagles had improved and I could incorporate them into my choreography. So keep in mind that being *able* to do something doesn't always mean that you *should* do it in competition, even though you should know and master all of the moves and their proper technique. You should always highlight your best skating when you skate for an audience.

4

Lunges

Lunges are a great move not often used in skating. A good lunge held for a long time will definitely get a crowd's reaction. Audiences appreciate the difficulty. However, lunges don't have to be held for very long to be useful in your choreography. In this chapter I will give you tips on how to do strong forward and backward lunges.

Starting Out

You should stretch before you begin working on lunges. Lunges require additional flexibility in the quadriceps, glutes, and hip flexors (the muscles that connect your upper thighs to your lower abdomen). Making sure you are loose will help you avoid injury. One good stretch for lunges is the standing quad stretch, in which you stand and hold your free foot or ankle. Your heel should touch your rear as you work to press your free thigh forward. To get the most out of the stretch, keep your knees close together. (See chapters 21 and 22 for additional stretches and warm-ups.)

Forward Lunge

After you have warmed up, take a forward stroke. As you lower to the ice on your skating leg, flex your free foot and let your free leg fall to the ice in a controlled motion. In a lunge, the side of your back boot will be gliding over the ice instead of your blade. Your weight should be toward the middle of your skate on the forward foot and your thigh should be about parallel with the ice (figure 4.1).

As you practice, be careful not to let your front knee extend beyond your toe or collapse to either side. Think of keeping your skating knee over your ankle. Your free leg should be straight, with your toe pointed once it is on the ice. When I do lunges, I feel my free foot gliding on the side of the boot, with pressure on the inside of the ball of my foot. You may want to invest in some boot covers if you practice the lunge a lot so that you don't ruin your boot's leather.

Your chest should be lifted, with your shoulders back. You'll know that you are in a good position if you think and feel that your neck is long. Your chest should be slightly forward over your skating leg (the front leg). If you keep your chest too far back, you will not be able to get as low in the position as necessary. At the same time, press down on your hips and lift up out of your waist. Even if you change your arms, it's still basically the same position. I always work to keep my shoulders back no matter how I might vary the move for choreography purposes.

As you come up out of the position, take a deep breath and use it to help you get up (figure 4.2). It is much nicer to come up without using your hands

Figure 4.1 Forward lunge.

Figure 4.2 A deep breath can help you lift up out of the postion without losing a nice line.

to press against your knee, instead lifting up with your body. If you find that you have to use your hands to come up, maybe you shouldn't hold the lunge as long or so low. You may need to come up a little bit because your muscles aren't able to hold that depth comfortably. Work to come up gracefully so that the move appears to be easy, no matter how difficult it may feel!

Backward Lunge

The backward lunge has the same look and technique of the forward lunge, except you are going backward. As you go into the back lunge, lift your free leg and flex your foot. Then bend your skating knee and let your free leg extend back as you lower yourself, pointing your toe once you're in position (figure 4.3). The most common problem in attempting back lunges is catching the skate on the ice instead of allowing the boot to glide over it as the lunge begins. Be careful of this because you can twist your ankle or jam it into your boot as the blade catches.

As with the forward lunge, watch that your front knee is not beyond your big toe and keep your balance over the middle of your skate. Remember to press your hips to the ice, with your chest back and neck long and lifted to create a beautiful line.

Figure 4.3 In the back lunge, the back boot glides over the ice.

Lunge Variations

Lunges shouldn't be static, and they don't have to be slow and graceful. They can be done in a jazzy program with both knees bent as opposed to just one. Instead of creating a long line, you can make them a fast and upbeat movement as well, going down into them and up out of them quickly in part of a footwork sequence. I've often done lunges from one end of the ice to the other, changing the position halfway through. For example, I would do an Ina Bauer into a lunge or a lunge into an Ina Bauer. It gives the move a little variation that can make it look fresh. I've also used them into jumps. I used to do back lunges into a jump or a back shoot the duck into Lutzes. It requires a lot of strength, and it is difficult to make it consistent, but you can do lunges in a variety of ways to keep the movement interesting. Often a basic move can have more impact than a harder one, so work on lunges and experiment with them.

Part 2
Mastering Spins

In the next two sections we will discuss specific freestyle moves. Although dancers and synchronized skaters do not need triple jumps, the tips and techniques in the coming chapters apply to all skaters. And when we discuss dance and synchro moves, there will also be techniques that apply to all skaters.

In this section we will focus specifically on spins, giving you the tips you need to make your spins faster and more centered. Each chapter will increase your skill level in the forward and backward spins, and I will also provide a few variations that you may try to help get your creative juices flowing. Chapter 8 will focus specifically on spin variations, providing key points to think of when trying spins like the layback or Biellmann.

There are a few general things to keep in mind as you work on all spins. Many skaters complain that they do not like to practice spins because it makes them dizzy. I still get dizzy from spins, but it is important to practice them because you adjust to the feeling through practice. You can learn ways to combat the dizzy feeling. For example, in the show "Footloose on Ice" I am lifted into a one-handed Detroiter. I have to stay straight like a board in the air, so I really concentrate on keeping my stomach muscles tight. I come out of the spin and go into a double Axel. I am usually so dizzy that I have to focus on something and then go into the jump. Luckily, there is a trash can in that scene, so as I come out of the spin I stare at the trash can and turn into my double Axel. If I didn't do that, I am sure that I would be completely off balance. Finding something stable to look at as you exit a spin may help you to find your center of balance.

Your coach may have used the word *centering* when describing spins. When we use this term, we mean that the spin stays in one spot and does not pivot away from its starting point. Learning to center a spin will help you to generate an upright axis for jumps and for ice dancing twizzles. As you practice all of your spins, try hard to stay centered and steady. If you are loose, you're probably going to go off center and travel. Stomach muscles are the most important in all of skating because you use them to keep your core straight. If you are up in the air in a jump or are spinning on the ice, you need your stomach muscles to be tight in order to stay centered. Practicing spins daily will also help.

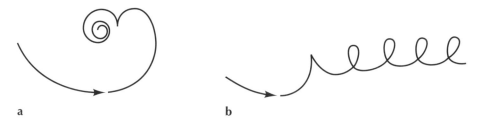

a   b

Compare ice patterns for *(a)* a centered spin and *(b)* an uncentered spin.

In all spins, if you try to find your balance point on your blade and work to maintain it, you will have better luck with centering your spins. In most spins, I feel that I'm spinning near the front of my blade. I'm not on my toe pick, but I am spinning just below it and working to keep that point stable as I spin by using my standing leg and my stomach muscles to press into the ice.

Good spins do take practice, but they can be very exciting when they are done well. If you follow my tips and work correctly, by the end of this section you will be spinning faster and stronger and you will have the increased knowledge of centering and alignment that is needed for jumps and more difficult skating moves. Remember to have fun with spins and explore to find out what variations you can do!

5

Scratch Spins

Scratch spins are one of my favorite spins because they are fast and can really make a statement. I usually start my spin practices with the back scratch because it is the same position needed in the air for jumps. Although the forward and backward scratch spins are the most basic of the spins, don't discount them. A fast scratch will always earn an extra round of applause. In this chapter I give you some tips on the basic spin entrance, the forward scratch spin, and the back spin, as well as a few variations that you can try on your own.

Scratch Spin Concepts

All of the entrances and exits for spins in the following chapters are written for skaters who jump and spin counterclockwise. If you jump or spin clockwise, reverse the instructions—for example, if the instructions say to start on the left foot, start on the right foot instead.

Forward spins have a variety of entrances. Most people do either the back crossover entrance or the forward inside three-turn entrance. The back crossover entrance is very common because it gives you the force and speed you need to make the spin fast and tight. On the last cross, wind up and bend your standing leg as the crossed-under leg is stretched beneath (figure 5.1). Let your upper body twist from your waist to the right so that your left hand is almost over your right foot.

Figure 5.1 Winding up on the last cross in preparation for the scratch spin.

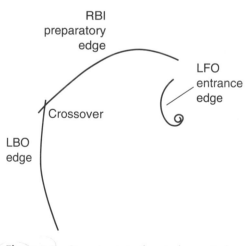

Figure 5.2 Stepping into the circle created on the ice.

On the crossover, remember to really push through with the free leg. The entrance should not just be a cross with a relaxed pickup of the free foot from the ice. If you just pick it up, you will not have the force you need to spin. You need an assertive push-through with the free leg to keep you strong and in a good position. Spins and jumps require speed and power, even in a slow section of your program, so really push into your spin to make it more exciting.

As you step into the spin, step into the circle that you've created (figure 5.2). Many skaters step forward into their spins in the same line they have created with their back crossovers. Your windup should continue and increase the depth of your edge so that when you step forward, you are stepping *into* the circle you've created, not *on* it. As you begin to spin, open your arms to the sides so that your shoulders and hips are square to your skating leg. At the same time, stand up straight. Straightening into the knee helps the spin to gain force and velocity (we will talk more about this later).

Forward Scratch

For a basic scratch spin, begin with the standard spin preparation. As you step forward and into your spin, your left arm should feel as if it is leading the way for the rest of your body. Katarina Witt and I tease each other about who can spin the fastest. She likes to step into the spin with her standing leg bent; she says that it makes the spin faster. I like to step into the spin with a straight standing leg (figure 5.3). If you are bending your knee, there is a chance that your rear will stick out and slow your momentum. Katarina has learned how to avoid that, but as you begin to work on it, practice with a straight standing leg. Eventually, you may find variations that will work better for your body.

As the spin catches, keep your arms out to your sides and a little in front of you to maintain your balance. Your elbows should always be a little higher than your wrists to create an attractive, stretched position. Many skaters start with their hands and arms too high. Try to feel that your back muscles are pulling down and your hands are pressing down as the spin starts.

As the spin's rotation tightens, make a circle with your hands at navel level, then pull your hands into your body. You should pull in so that your arms are almost parallel to the ice. It should be about where your ribs come together—where you would do the Heimlich maneuver. Then push your hands down so that they are low and close to your body. The muscles beneath your shoulder blades (your lats) will tighten in resistance while your triceps tighten as if they were squeezing something very heavy. As you do this, remember to keep your shoulders down and your abdomen in and lifted.

Figure 5.3   Stepping into the spin with the standing leg straight.

Your right leg will be forward and stretched at about a 45-degree angle to your front. As you pull it in to cross at your knee, lead with the heel of your boot so that the side of your right skate will touch your knee (figure 5.4). As you do this, think of closing your knees and pulling the thighs together. When you are first learning, you are often told to put the leg to the side. It's hard to cross over because it should actually be to the front of you and slightly to the side. One way to find this position is to keep your free hip closed. If you think of that it will be difficult to put the leg too far to the side. It will also increase your spin's speed and will be a more attractive position. Slide the free leg down the standing leg so that your legs are low and crossed (figure 5.5). As you do this, feel that your toe is pointed and your belly and rear are tucked and tight. This will help to keep your spin centered.

As you feel your momentum slow and think that you can't rotate any more, you should be preparing for your exit. For any sort of turn, prepare for your exit a quarter to a half of a turn before the exit so that you can bend into your knees and push out. It is much nicer to come out of a spin or jump with

Figure 5.4 Cross the free foot in front of the skating leg at the knee, then slide it down.

Figure 5.5 Ending position for the front scratch spin.

speed than slowing to a stop, so you need to really use your skating leg and your knee to bend and push out. Although there are many variations of the scratch spin, if you are doing a cross-leg spin you should step onto the foot you have crossed over, in this case your right foot. Pick up your left foot and use your free leg to pull out of the spin.

I like to do quick stops out of scratch spins. They are effective for a change in music or for the end of a program because they are exciting. As you are turning, push your free leg forward with a pointed toe and pick it into the ice. It feels like a little kick with the free leg, and the toe pick stops you. If you push your foot out properly, you will actually hear the heel of your free leg hit the toe pick of your skating foot. A fast stop can add a nice punch to your spin ending.

Back Scratch

All of the principles for the forward spin apply to the back spin. The only difference is that you will be spinning on your right foot instead of the left. I usually start it with a forward inside three turn. As I prepare to turn, I wind slightly more to the right than I would for a normal three, allowing my left hand to cross over my tracing and my torso to wind to the right (figure 5.6a). Then I unwind for the three and the spin catches (figure 5.6b).

The exit of the spin is always a little difficult because it can look as if you have to hop out of it. Think *up and out* with your free leg as you exit. If you think of taking your free leg wide and check against it with your upper body to stop the momentum of the spin, keeping your abdomen and chest lifted, you will be able to glide out of the spin on an outside edge. The ending of this spin should stop the rotation without looking jerky, so remember to tighten your abdominal muscles to control the force. Another variation is to step onto the crossed-over leg on an inside edge for the finish. However, it is a good idea to first practice the outside edge exit. This will be the same exit you will need for your jumps, so it is a good position to master.

Scratch Variations

There are as many variations of each of these spins as you can think of. The first one to try is the scratch spin–change–back scratch. This variation is not commonly practiced, but it may help you to understand the feeling of a sit–change–back sit. You should begin with a basic scratch spin. Place your right foot next to your left. (You will have to uncross your right foot to do this.) Bend both legs and push onto your right foot so that you are now spinning on your right foot.

You can also try a back scratch–change–scratch. From your regular back scratch spin, uncross your left foot and place it next to your right. Bend your

a   b

Figure 5.6 The back scratch spin: *(a)* preparation and *(b)* spin position.

knees and push onto your left foot. Your right leg will swing around to the front so that you finish in your regular scratch spin position.

Other variations include bringing your arms over your head and bringing your hands to your chin so that your head releases back. For both of these spins, instead of pressing your arms down, pull them straight up. You will follow the path of your spin. As you bring your hands over your head, remember to keep your shoulders down. Your hands should finish slightly forward from the crown of your head. If you choose to do the head-back spin, lift your head from your chin so that your neck is long and not broken in its position. You want to achieve the illusion that your head is at a 90-degree angle, but your neck should be completely stretched on all sides. Your hands will be under your chin with your elbows lifted and parallel to the ice.

The scratch spin and back scratch will be used in variations for all of the other spins, so remember to work on them. A good scratch spin will make you look like a blur and will be a very exciting addition to any program ending.

6

Sit Spins

Recently a skater came up to me and asked me to demonstrate a cannonball sit spin. I had not heard that name before, but she told me that a cannonball sit involved pulling your head to your leg or your leg to your head. I didn't want to try it until I understood how it should be done, so I smiled and said, "Let me see yours." Her coach was standing there and we both smiled knowingly to each other as she tried to show us the position. She was sort of half sitting and half trying to pull her head to her knee. The coach turned to me and said, "Nancy, you could do that!" When I tried it, I was actually too low, but she was not low enough. If your sit spin doesn't sit, it can look like a bent-over, bent-down spin—it's not really a sit. You must sit low to the ice, and almost always must do the spin while you are moving. This chapter will expand your knowledge of sit spins, explain how a back sit is done, and give you a few position variations to try.

Sit Spin Concepts

When I was injured in 1994, the doctors asked me to demonstrate a sit spin position off the ice. I couldn't do it off the ice because my knee was too swollen, but for some reason I could do it on the ice. The centripetal force of the spin pulled me down into the position and didn't hurt my knee. The centripetal and centrifugal forces in a good sit spin should not only help you to get into the sit but also help you to get out of it, and a good sit spin should arrive easily in the sitting position.

In both the forward and the backward sit you must get low to the ice, but there is such a thing as being too low. You want to be low enough that your thigh is parallel to the ice. Some skaters go all the way down so that the rear is resting on the boot and the knee is pointing straight up. There is nothing technically wrong in this approach and you may already be doing your sit spin this way; but if the spin is still relatively new to you, don't push for that kind of depth at this point. Above all, a sit spin should not look labored, so no matter how low you go you should not have to use your arms to come up. The force of spinning should help you come up, just as it should help you go down. In show numbers, many skaters go lower and use their arms to come up. Nicole Bobek does her sit spin this way in shows, and it is awesome. However, when you are just learning, try to keep the spin at a comfortable depth and learn not to use your hands to come up.

Forward Sit

As you begin to practice the sit spin, you may fall a lot until you comfortably find the position. Don't worry about it. There are always some moves that take a little longer to learn, but once you have them they will always be yours. The basic entrance for a sit spin is the same entrance you use for a scratch spin. You will do a back crossover with a strong windup away from the circle. As you step in, remember to step into your circle, not on the same line as your last cross. At the same time, push off your right leg, allowing the leg to straighten and swing in a wide arc from the back to the front (figure 6.1a). I like to step in first to feel the standing spin position and then come down all at once into the sit instead of stepping in and coming down at the same time. If you just step into the spin and try to bend into the sit at the same time, you are most likely going to be out of control and not be able to stay and sit, or not be able to go down as far, or fall right over because you just don't have control. When you step, step in with your standing knee slightly bent and the foot will come around in a wide arc. Then, as it comes around, you will go down into the sit position. The force of swinging your free leg quickly from the back to the front will give you force and speed. Both your free leg and your arms will go around and down and will help you to go faster into the spin. Remember to keep your weight centered on the ball of your skating foot. At this point, you should be sitting close to the ice with your left leg bent at about a 90-degree angle (figure 6.1b).

As you spin, your upper body will probably lean slightly forward, but you should still feel that your waist and ribs are lifted and your shoulders are back. Unless you are trying to do a variation, I think it is much neater and easier to stay in a good position for a long time if you bend your free leg around in front of you. This helps to keep your legs closed in a nicer position. The inside edge of your foot should be facing up and pointed. If your foot

a   b

Figure 6.1   Front sit spin: *(a)* preparation and *(b)* sit position.

is facing down, it is less attractive and keeps you from sitting as low as you need to.

When you feel your momentum slow and you are ready to end the spin, lean forward with your upper body and push forward and up. Your rear may rise a little bit as you do this, but you should feel that your hips press forward and your abdominal muscles contract to lift you into a straight scratch spin. This action will bring you back to vertical and will give you extra momentum. In the past, judges took points off if you used your hands to push on your leg to come up. It's much nicer if you can come up without them. So to get out of the spin, you can use your arms to lift you out and up but without pressing your hands on your legs. As you go into your regular scratch, bring your free leg to your knee and bring your arms into the rounded position in front of your belly button so that you finish with a fast scratch.

Back Sit

I prefer the back sit to the forward sit. It may be that my right leg is a little stronger because it's my landing leg. I like to do the back change sit as opposed to practicing the back sit alone, although the back sit may also be done from a forward inside three turn as we did with the back scratch. The back sit position is not really any different from the forward sit. When they are done with a change between, the back sit and forward sit should look exactly the same.

To begin practicing, do a regular sit spin. After a few revolutions, open your arms, but stay low to the ice (figure 6.2a). Put your free leg (in this case, the right) on the ice on an inside edge. At this point, transfer your weight onto your right leg, bending into the sit spin, and press and push into the ice with your left leg (your new free leg) so that you can lift it off the ice in a low turned-out position (figure 6.2b). On the transition, imagine that you are in a room with a very low ceiling; if you stand up while pushing onto the right foot, you will bump your head on the ceiling. Therefore, try to keep your body at the same level so that you do not lose any momentum in standing and resitting for the back sit.

From this point, remember all of the things from your forward sit, including spinning on the ball of your foot, keeping your back and free leg straight, and pointing your toe. When you feel your momentum slow, again lean forward to rise forward and out of the spin. Remember to try not to use your hands to press on your knees to come out of the spin. Finish in a fast back spin.

a   b

Figure 6.2 Change and back sit: *(a)* arms open, preparing to change legs in transition from the front sit to the back sit; and *(b)* back sit position.

Sit Spin Variations

The sit spin offers several variations. One such variation is the flying sit spin. This is not a spin you should practice if you are just mastering a sit spin because you must feel confident and comfortable with your sit spin to add a jump before it. Begin with a back crossover entrance that finishes with a strong windup. As you unwind and step into your circle, swing your arms back and bend deeply into your left (skating) knee (figure 6.3a). Your free leg should be stretched behind you. As you jump, swing your right leg out and around, straighten your left leg, and jump straight up into the air. Once in the air, bend your left leg beneath you and bring your right leg forward (figure 6.3b). Your free leg should be bent about

a

b   c

Figure 6.3   Flying sit spin: *(a)* entrance, *(b)* in air position, and *(c)* landing.

90 degrees because you want it to look higher than it is. It should look like a sit spin when you are flying. In the air, you will need quick reflexes in your thigh to tuck your free leg under. Your arms should be straight out to your sides. When you land, your arms will come forward. To get a stable landing, you should land the spin first and then spin—don't land it and start spinning at the same time. It should look that way because it happens so fast, but actually your leg lands and then your free leg will be outside just as if you're going into a sit spin, and then you pull down with the arm and free leg. Finish with a regular sit spin (figure 6.3c).

One variation of the flying sit is the flying change sit. For this spin, you will change your leg positions in the air. This spin is a little harder, so Evy used to teach it to us at the boards. We would begin holding the boards, standing on the left foot. Then we would jump and bend both legs at the same time. Practicing at the boards is a good way to learn the timing of the switch of the free legs. To change, you bring your free leg (right leg) through almost as if it's an Axel, but it is straight. To switch, you tuck your left leg beneath you faster. As you tuck the left leg, the right leg is coming up, and then it flicks out. It is sort of like riding a bike. For a split second, both legs are bent. This will give you a great deal of force when you come down and you will have a fast back sit spin.

Another, simpler variation is the bent-leg sit spin. For this spin, your free leg will be bent, turned in at the side. You should feel almost as if you are pulling the leg up, lifting with the ankle and the front of the boot. This can also be done with a slight sideways lean.

You can also try a back sit–sit combination. From your back sit, step onto your left foot, swinging your free leg out and around wide again just as you would do on the forward sit. On the transition from your right foot to your left foot, stay as low to the ice as you can. You have to come up a little to get the stretch and pull, but don't come up too far—it's distracting and counter-productive.

Importance of Quality

As we begin to work on these more difficult spin combinations, keep in mind that they should match whatever music you use. A simple sit or back sit may be better than a variation simply for variation's sake. Skating is about quality. So work to make all of your basics as strong as possible—then, if you come up with a variation that is strong and goes with your music, include it. However, don't do it just to be different—do it because it is really good.

7

Camel Spins

When I first began working on camel spins with Evy Scotvold, he used to call me "the sundial" because I spun so slowly. Over the years I have learned that you have to be centered to have a fast, effective camel spin. It's hard to learn, but believe me, it can be learned. In this chapter, we will discuss proper technique for both a forward and back camel and learn a few variations, including the change camel and the flying camel. Although camel spins take a little bit of courage and a lot of speed to do well, they are very dynamic spins and may soon be one of your favorites.

Camel Spin Concepts

Through practice with my camel spins, I've learned that the best way to control them is to avoid rushing into the final spin position. The trick is the timing. To do a proper camel without falling over my toe or bobbing up and down or traveling down the ice as I try to spin, I think of not going into the spin. As I go into the spin, I push my free foot down and out and then slowly lift it into the air without dropping my upper body. It should take half a turn to a turn for the free leg to finish in its full position in the air. In practicing the spin that way, I found that the spin was not only more centered but also faster.

When you are first learning camel spins, many of the same principles that we discussed in the spiral chapter (chapter 2) apply. Once you learn your body, your center of gravity, and how to hold the spin, you may make changes to the position to match the music. However, to learn it and to be able to find your own center of gravity, keep in mind that the shoulders should be back, your head should be lifted, and your center and torso should be firm. Remember, abdominal strength is crucial to spin effectively.

Forward Camel

Just as in a scratch spin or a sit spin, you will begin a forward camel from a series of back crossovers. On the last crossover, wind from your waist so that your body turns away from your circle. Bend your right knee and straighten your left (crossed-under) leg. Think about stepping into the circle with your left arm in front and your chest up (figure 7.1a). You will use your left side to lead you into the circle. Unlike your circle in a scratch spin or a sit spin, in the camel your circle from the back crossover into the spin will look like two lobes. You don't step back into the circle you created in the back crossovers. You actually step out on a deep outside edge into the spin. Some skaters, such as professional skater Craig Heath, are so good at this back edge to forward camel transition that they can actually turn the camel on a deep outside edge. Craig is able to put a hat on the ice and actually do his camel around it. It's beautiful!

As you push off your right leg, allow it to follow you around and slowly get into position (figure 7.1b). If you take your time, your free leg will slowly rise into a clean position and you will arrive in a balanced place on

a   b

Figure 7.1 Camel spin: *(a)* push into the spin, *(b)* slow lift of the free leg, and

the ball of your foot for the spin. If you step and push, lifting your leg in the air at the same time, your hip will not be over your standing foot and you will likely plummet forward. If you are too far forward on your blade, your instinct will be to pull your chest back up and say, "I'm going to save it!" That actually makes you slow. If you are in a test or at competition, you have to turn a minimum of six to eight times, depending on the spin, and it is brutal if you are turning slowly. A proper entrance will help to assure that you spin steadily. If you stay centered, you will spin faster. When you are spinning, remember to keep your free leg straight, turned out, and pointed. At the same time, keep your chin and chest lifted (figure 7.1c).

You have a few options for arm position. You can be in a position with one arm forward. If I have one arm forward, I go on an outside edge. It took me a long time to learn to do it, but I think it's a beautiful position. Another option is to keep the arms square to your upper body. This centers you and can also be a very controlled, solid position. Some skaters put both arms back, and it looks as if they are holding their rears. If you are supposed to do it, it can look good, but some people look as if they have put their arms back because they didn't know what else to do. Even if you keep your shoulders back and have your hands more toward the front, on the thighs, the position can look very good. The important thing is to pick a position and commit to it.

When preparing to exit a camel, bring your free leg down next to your standing leg and stand up to push out of the spin. If you decide to do a scratch spin to finish the spin, you should stand up first before you begin to spin so that you are able to find your balance and do a fast spin to end.

c

(c) spin position, which varies slightly with each skater.

Back Camel

Back camels may be done from a three-turn entrance or from a camel–change–camel. The back three-turn entrance is very hard. Once you feel more comfortable on all of your back spins, you may want to try them without the camel and change before it. Some skaters can do back spins from back spirals, dropping their free leg into the

a   b

Figure 7.2   Camel–change–camel: *(a)* from a front camel, *(b)* bring legs together,

circle to begin the spin. This is also a great entrance. However, let's begin
with the camel–change–camel.

Start with a regular camel spin (figure 7.2a). From there, bring your feet
together, but don't stand up (figure 7.2b). Keeping your body square to the
ice, lift your new free leg (the left) into the air (figure 7.2c). If you began with
your left arm forward, swing it to the side on the transition, and bring it back
and your right arm forward as your left leg lifts into the air. Just as you did
with the forward camel, take your time to get into position so that you will
be able to control it. In the back spin transition, your free leg is down
switching feet and then passing through as opposed to around. Remember
to lift the leg with control from the stomach and buttocks (do not kick the leg
up). In the spin, remember to keep your chest and head lifted and create a
nice line with your free leg in the air. To exit, you can either finish with a fast
back scratch or put your free leg down and push to come out of the spin into
a stretch.

Camel Variations

Once you feel comfortable with the forward and backward camel spin, you
may also try the back camel–change–forward camel. Do a regular back

c

then *(c)* rise out of the knee into position.

camel. On the transition, bring your free leg down to your skating leg, keeping your upper body low. Then push onto your forward camel. You will do a three turn to begin spinning. Finish with a regular scratch spin or push to come out of it. As you work on this spin, try to keep it moving from the three spin positions smoothly. It is very easy to stall on the transition, making the spin lose speed. Ideally, you should be able to do a camel–change–back camel–change–camel if you keep your momentum going and really use the ice to push hard on each change.

The hardest of all flying spins is the flying camel. In a flying camel, you must transfer your horizontal motion into a centered spin. Begin with back crossovers and wind up for the spin as you would for a scratch spin. Bend your right knee and pull your arms back as you step forward and jump (figure 7.3a). As you stroke onto your left foot, think of stepping out of your circle. You will actually land almost on top of where you were, but you should feel as if you are jumping out. Spring into the air, swinging your right leg in a wide arc to the side (figure 7.3b). At the same time, your left leg will lift off the ice and swing in a wide arc to the back (figure 7.3c). For a split second you will hang in the air parallel to the ice.

As you work on the flying camel, remember that it's supposed to fly: it's called a flying camel, not a hop with a switch of the legs. So your leg should really lift off the ice to give you height. Remember to keep your chest and back lifted and open as you are flying. As you land, check your left shoulder back to help stabilize the landing. Your right toe pick will touch down and your left leg will swing counterclockwise so that you are now doing a back camel (figure 7.3d). Finish with a regular back spin.

Two other spins I will briefly mention are the flying camel sit, or death drop, and the butterfly. Both the death drop and the butterfly are momentum moves, so they will be easier on the ice with speed. However, when you are first learning them, practice on the floor until you have the feel for the flying aspect of each spin.

Not too long ago, Brian Boitano, who has what I think is technically the best and most exciting spin, taught me a new way to do the death drop. He

Figure 7.3   Flying camel: *(a)* entrance, *(b)* spring into air, *(c)* further movement in air, and

told me that I needed to go into the death drop fast, as fast as I would go into a triple. Instead of taking off from a back inside edge, Brian switches to a back outside. It is almost the position for an Axel. Step into it as you would for an Axel, but pull your shoulders and arms back and both of your feet up when you are in the air. It feels like a spring and looks sort of like a butterfly lifting both of its wings up (figure 7.4). When you come down, if it is big enough, you may not be able to do it on one foot because it is very hard to control with the added speed. Brian has said that this way is more of a trick, and the trick is to get that huge height and the layout on top. He could probably control it if he had to, but it will most likely be hard to control when you are first learning it.

The normal entrance is to stay on the right back inside edge and step into the circle. As you step, your arms should be back and straight so that you can get the most from them. In the air, your arms will come up and out to pull your hands and shoulders back. The right leg should kick up. The left leg is especially important—it tends to lag behind because you are pushing off it. You need to really kick it up. For a second, both legs will straighten in the air. As you land, you will whip into the sit spin, and later exit. You won't have as much speed and spring with this approach as you would have with Brian's method because you don't have the speed and the back outside edge to give you the extra lift. For some reason, from the back inside edge you are

c   d

(d) landing into back camel.

blocked, preventing you from getting such a huge jump. However, you can still get the same effect by pulling your arms and legs up at the same time. In doing so, you will be able to spin the landing for competition while still achieving the exciting effect of Brian's death drop.

In the butterfly, the skater takes off from two feet and scissors the legs in the air by kicking the free leg backward, then executing the same movement with the skating leg. I didn't learn this move until later in my career. I consider it to be more of a trick than a spin,

Figure 7.4 In-air position of the death drop.

but it can be very effective in show programs. When I was learning it, I began on the floor. With my back flat and my chest parallel to the ground, I would stand on both feet and swing my arms back and forth like an airplane. Then, with my knees, I would bend from side to side just enough so that I could push off. I'm on an inside edge for the takeoff, so my weight transfers to my right foot. As I spring, my head and lower body swing down toward my left leg. It is a swooping action. My head and shoulders pull back to come up and go against the downswinging motion. My legs lift up as my upper body comes up so that when I am almost turning left, where I was, my right foot lifts off and my left foot kicks up to follow it. In the air, my arms and legs spread wide so that it looks like a butterfly (figure 7.5). To stand up when you land, you need to swoop your head down to start and then pull your upper body back up so that you can stand.

Figure 7.5 In-air position of the butterfly.

To me, the death drop feels and looks more the way a butterfly would fly because your arms and legs go together. The butterfly spin is more like a domino, with one leg lifting and then the other. Butterflies don't fly this way, but this is how the move feels in the air.

Camel spins may be done with countless changes of position and variations in the arms and legs, so be creative. Try a camel–sit–back sit–back scratch, or a sit–back camel–forward camel–back sit, or any other variations you can come up with. You now have all of the tools you need to be creative with the basic spins.

8

Spin Variations

In the past few chapters, we have covered all of the basic spins you will need to perform countless combinations. In this chapter, we will look at spins unlike the scratch, sit, camel, or any of their variations. We will discuss spins such as the layback, the Biellmann, illusions, and a few other fun variations. Some of these spins may more naturally fit your body than others, and you may even come up with variations of the variation. It is always fun to try moving in new ways, but work carefully as you are trying out some of these moves. If you are attempting these spins for the first time, work under a coach's supervision. Keep in mind all of the basic techniques from earlier chapters, and remember that if it does not come naturally, maybe it shouldn't, or perhaps you need to train your body by stretching in new ways. Work in ways that fit your body. Who knows, you may one day have a new variation named after you!

Spin Variation Concepts

Most variations are born either because a skater can't do a move and must modify it for his or her body or because he or she can do something unique. For me, the layback was always very difficult. I began doing a sort of sideways spin because I couldn't lean back. The position really hurt my back, and my back has continued to hurt me since I was 15. It is less painful now, but that is only because I broke two bones in my back (not recommended!), which gave me greater flexibility for the spin. The vertebra has knobs. As I practiced the layback, the doctors believe that the muscle that wraps around the knobs rubbed them and they broke off. Now I am able to lean back, but I don't think that all of the years of pain were worth it. At the time that my back was in pain, layback variations were not really accepted. Finally, variations were permitted, but skaters didn't receive credit for them for years. It has changed in recent years, and we are now seeing skaters, such as Lucinda Ruh, who are able to do many different changes in position.

As I mentioned previously, I developed a sideways lean from the layback position. I start from a regular scratch spin. As I begin to spin, I lift up out of my waist on one side and lean in the other direction (figure 8.1). For example, I lift the left side so that I am leaning slightly to the right. My left arm extends into the air to follow the line. My right leg also extends to my side with the toe pointed. I look to the right to complete the line. The important thing with all variations is that you shouldn't do them for variation's sake. They should not only look good on you, but they should

Lucinda Ruh's "pancake sit spin" demonstrates the creativity that is possible with spin variations.

© J. Barry Mittan

Figure 8.1 Sideways leaning spin variation.

also go with your music and augment or showcase something that you can do well.

Layback

Although the layback is not my favorite spin, I have found a way to make it work for me, and I hope that it will help you too. The one trick I have learned is that as you go back, you need to lift up and out of your waist. If you just lean back, you're going to crunch your lower back, and that's not healthy. We're not really built to do this, so if you pick up your middle, you can separate your vertebrae to make room and make the transition a little easier. As you lean back, drop your chin back. If you try to keep your chin forward, your neck will be tense and you will feel stuck as you try to lean back. You need to let your head and chin stay in line as you extend back so that your head is in line with your spine (figure 8.2).

Before you attempt to do this spin on the ice, practice it at the boards. Stand with your hands on the boards or a counter or a chair. Once you can

Figure 8.2 Full layback position.

maintain this position without spinning, try taking it out onto the ice. The momentum of spinning will help to increase your position's range just as it did in the sit spin. The layback may be done from the scratch spin entrance we have talked about in previous chapters or the forward inside three-turn entrance. When you step into the spin, really hold it just as you would for a scratch spin first to find your balance. Instead of just going directly back into the spin, make a statement by holding a solid spin and then going back into the layback.

As you begin to lean back, lift up from the waist and the ribs. Push your hips slightly forward so that they are farther over the middle to the ball of your foot. This will also give you more room to extend and will protect your back. As the spin slows, use your abdominal muscles to help you come out of it and back to standing. You can either push out of the spin at this point or do a scratch spin.

You can use many different styles for the free foot. Some people like it close with a bent free leg, and some like the free leg straight with a turned-out toe. The main thing to keep in mind is that the toe should be pointed and your free leg should be in an attitude position. In an attitude, your lower leg and foot should be parallel to the ice. For some people, the flat position is difficult to achieve, so I recommend that you flex your foot. It sounds strange, and if you try it when you are just standing, it may look a little funny. However, when you are spinning it can help to keep it parallel to the ice. It is, of course, best to point it and keep your foot flat to the ice. Not everyone can do that, though, so it is better for your foot to be at least flat to the ice as opposed to pointed down.

Other variations relate to how your arms are positioned in the spin. It is most natural when you are first starting out for your arms to be in a circle above you. I like to have the hands at the level of my shoulders instead of at the level of my chest. It helps to rotate my shoulders back. That is the normal arm position—however, once you are comfortable in the layback position, you should do variations to change them. If I bring my arms sideways (figure 8.3), I feel as though I get back a little farther because the centrifugal force helps to pull me down. However, it is a little harder to get out of the position when you are ready to exit. Another variation that gives flair is to have one arm overhead and one in front during the spin. Experiment to see what feels natural to you.

Figure 8.3 A spin variation with the arms back.

Illusions

Another spin, which was surely created from a day of experimentation at the rink, is the illusion. In an illusion, the skater reaches toward the ice with the free side so that the hand touches the ice and the free leg reaches to the ceiling (figure 8.4). It is usually done from a back camel. Some skaters can do an illusion from a forward camel, but it is fairly rare. It is harder to get the momentum going on a forward illusion, making it more difficult. I usually begin it from a flying camel. Once I land the spin, I drop my right arm to the ice, trying to keep my body in a straight line. As I do this, I drop my head, tucking my chin in so that I fall forward. Most skaters only do a few of these because it is difficult to maintain the momentum. When you are ready to come out, pull your body back to vertical and either finish in a back scratch or push out on a back outside edge.

Figure 8.4   Illusion.

Biellmann Spin

Denise Biellmann stunned audiences when she created her own variation of the layback. The 1981 world champion reached back with her arms and pulled her leg over her head so that she created what resembled an egg shape with her upper body. Although very few people can actually do the full Biellmann, some skaters also do a sort of half-Biellmann in which they take the free leg from the arabesque position, reaching back with the right hand to pull the free right leg into the air behind them. I must stress that if your body does not want to do this position naturally, you should not force it. If you are somewhat comfortable in it, definitely practice off ice first, and make sure that you are fully stretched out—specifically in your hips, thighs, back, shoulders, and arms—before you attempt the position. As you try it, remember to keep your leg behind you. Your knee should be rolled in so that it looks more attractive. If you practice this and you are wearing your skates, be careful about reaching back for your blade. To avoid cutting yourself on the blade, you need to grab on the underside of your blade rather than over the blade.

© J. Barry Mittan

Many skaters perform this unique spin variation created by Denise Biellmann.

Above all, as you work on variations, keep in mind that everyone is built differently. What may work for others may not work for you. Don't be afraid to experiment, but listen to your body. If you are not able to do a position comfortably after some practice, come up with a variation or try to make it comfortable for your body. It may mean that you will not be able to do the spin, but you may actually be able to create a spin that will amaze audiences and that everyone will want to try.

Work on spins that you already know how to do. Play games. Challenge yourself to see how many revolutions of a spin you can do or how many different arm or leg positions you can come up with. Practice what you know, and sometimes, when you think you've actually made a mistake or when you least expect it, you will find a move that is all yours.

Part 3

Nailing Jumps

"Will you watch my double flip?" a sweet seven-year-old recently asked me. I said, "Well, sure, but how about if I see your single first?" because I had never seen her skate. She looked so distraught, as if wondering, *Why would you want to see the single? I want to show you the double.* Nonetheless, she did the single and it was OK, but there was no way that she could do a double from it. Her arms were not helping her to get the spring she needed for a double. I showed her how to do it and said, "Why don't you keep practicing your single, and at the end of the session I'll watch your double." By the end of the session the jump was about two inches higher, giving her more time to get around for the double.

In the introduction, I talked about my experience with returning to singles after I was already working on triples. As I said, it was a difficult process, but it was worth it because I really learned the basic principles of jumping, which I could then apply to all jumps. In the last few chapters we discussed spins. By now, you are familiar with the importance of abdominal muscles, finding your vertical axis, and speed to make an element work. With that knowledge, you are now ready to work on your jumps! In the coming chapters we will continue to examine how your vertical axis plays a role in your jumps. We will also look at the biomechanics needed for single, double, and triple jumps. For the ambitious among you, the skills we will discuss are also applicable to quads. All of the jumps that we will discuss in this section have certain similarities. As you work on jumping, we will often discuss the takeoff (jump entrance), landing, speed, and timing. Before we move forward with the individual jumps, let's take a look at a few of the basic concepts.

Jump Takeoffs

I often get very frustrated when I watch skating on television. If a jump has gone wrong, commentators tend to focus on what has happened in the air—but usually something has gone wrong with the takeoff. If a jump is tilted in the air, it is a reaction to an action—and takeoff and preparation are what cause problems in the jump or spin. It is very rare to see a skater who is perfectly straight in the air suddenly lean. Occasionally, if you are in a show, the spotlights may get into your eyes and throw you off. However, if that is not the case, you will most likely find by reviewing a tape of the performance, or by going back and looking at the takeoff tracing on the ice, that something went wrong at that point that caused the reaction. You may see that your toe picked in crooked, or you were leaning on the takeoff, or your arms didn't come through correctly. So you almost always find the cause of the problem through examination of the takeoff.

On any jump, you need to remember to use not only your knees and your upper body to lift you into the air, but also your feet. Often you will see jumpers who jump only from the knees up. On a toe jump, your toe should toe in on the way up to help lift you into the air as if it were a pole vault. If you toe in too late, you won't be able to get the proper spring. On an edge jump, you need to use your feet to create the edge that lifts you into the air. If you jump all the way through your feet, your jump will be higher and your feet will be cleaner in the air.

Brian Boitano and I were talking about jumps one day and he told me that on his spread eagle into his triple 'Tano Lutz, he counts, "One one-thousand, two one-thousand, three one-thousand, go!" He does that because skating is all about timing. Even though Brian is incredibly strong, the actual lift into a jump is about timing. His strength helps him to make things bigger, but the timing is really what makes the jump happen efficiently.

Jumps also require speed to make them not only exciting, but to give them greater spring. A lot of times people are afraid to go fast because they are afraid to fall. You may as well go for it—we all eventually fall, and jumping assertively gives you a much better chance of executing it properly.

One of the most common things that can go wrong in jumps is that your arms pull in too early, ahead of the rest of your body. The timing of the arms is very important. How tightly you pull them in will determine whether you are going to do a single, double, or triple. The position of the arms is also very important. On the flip, the Lutz, and the toe, the arm has to be directly behind you so that you have force to propel yourself straight into the air. I tell skaters that if you put your arm all the way behind you, you can feel a pinch in your scapula because there is tension underneath your shoulder blade. It is also very important that you keep the shoulders down. If your arm is too high, instead of coming straight through with your arms close to your center of balance, you're likely going to scoop them up. If it is already coming from a high place, you will scoop it too hard and too high and it will throw you sideways at an angle. We will discuss the arms for each

Tight in-air jump position.

jump in the coming chapters, but keep in mind that the arms should help lift you into the air. So if they come through too high or too late, you will probably have problems in the air.

When you are in the air, your arms should be close to your body and your feet should be low and tight. The only skater that I know has been successful with wrapping the free leg is Midori Ito. It must have been something with her body type that made it work, but most of us are not able to wrap, nor do we want to. If you think about a top, the fastest it is going to spin is when everything is balanced directly over itself and everything is in tight. If your leg is sticking out, it's going to slow you down. To avoid this, Evy gave me an exercise for single jumps with keeping my feet side by side. At first it felt very awkward, but it did prevent me from wrapping my jumps, and when I returned to crossing them they were definitely tighter. If you can eventually do singles and then doubles with your feet side by side, triples should be easier.

Jump Landings

While the takeoff for a jump is very important, a proper landing is also crucial. Many skaters have a very high free leg on the way out of their jump.

Proper jump landing.

A high free leg can be beautiful if it is done well and the leg is behind you. For stability, I prefer to keep my free leg lower on the landing. If you are stable when you first land, there is less of a chance that you will fall, so I push my free leg down and point the toe. After I am on balance, my free leg naturally lifts a little more. No matter how you land, your free leg should be behind you and your upper body should be in equilibrium.

As you practice your jumps, try to do them as they are in your programs. Although it is important to do them in an informal, technical way, to get consistency and confidence you need to practice them with the entrance and exit you do in your program. The normal or so-called "standard" entrance may be slightly different from the way it appears in your program, so practice your jumps as you would perform them. Any jump that you include in your program should be consistent so that you have the confidence of being able to land them when you are in a performance. For me that meant being able to land each jump no less than 8 out of 10 times in a session.

Remember that all of the skills we discuss should be practiced off the ice before you take them on the ice. Many skaters learn to jump without ever jumping. They practice on the ground doing the jump entrance with a step into a back spin to learn the muscle memory of their rotational position. Others work on trampolines to feel the added spring that will be used for jumping. However you choose to work on your jumps off the ice, work steadily, with some supervision, and try to replicate the feeling you are working to create on the ice. Without further ado, let's get jumping!

9

Salchows

In this chapter we will discuss how to do single, double, and triple Salchows. The Salchow is one of three edge jumps; as such, it requires a strong commitment to the inside edge. Again, keep in mind during this and subsequent chapters that the instructions we provide will relate to those who jump counterclockwise. If you are left-handed or jump clockwise, remember to reverse all instructions—if the text says left, you should use your right, and so on.

Singles

There are several ways to prepare for a Salchow. The jump is initiated from a back left inside edge. Some skaters prefer to do a forward stroke into a mohawk. Others prefer a three turn or back crossovers. However you choose to get into the jump, keep in mind that a Salchow is an edge jump and you should take off from a single foot, riding the edge until your body is in the 3 o'clock position which takes you naturally into the jump. Some people take off with both feet on the ice. To me, that looks like a weird loop, and the jump is smaller and less effective. To learn the jump correctly you should take off from one edge.

I usually do the Salchow from a left outside three turn. If you do the Salchow this way, it is very important to remember to push into the turn. Many people sort of step into the turn, which does not give them any speed to propel them into the air. As you push, your right arm will be at a 12 o'clock position and your left arm will be at 6. Your arms will switch so that your left arm is in front of you at 12 and your right arm is behind you at 6 after the turn. As I bend into my standing leg (my left), my free leg and free arm (right) go to 3 o'clock. Then, as I bend into my left knee and spring into the air, my right arm and right leg move from 3 o'clock across my body to 9 o'clock (figure 9.1). Often, before I jump, I will remind myself of this combination: 6, 3, 9. This helps to confirm the pattern and positions my free leg and arm will move in before I jump.

As you spring from your left leg, your right knee should pull up and across your body as if you were walking diagonally up a step. It is very common for skaters to pass the leg through too close as the free leg passes from 3 o'clock to the 9 o'clock position. If you do that, your knees will be too tight and you will have nothing to jump into. In short, you will feel stuck. As you lift into the air, think of crossing your free leg wide and apart from your springing leg so that you will have something to jump into.

a   b

Figure 9.1 Single Salchow: *(a)* after the three turn, *(b)* free arm and leg moving to 3 o'clock,

Many skaters fall into the circle with their upper bodies before the Salchow. Usually this is because they have not been aggressive enough with the placement of the right arm. As you push into your Salchow, push your right arm directly forward so that it is in line with your skating foot and moving in the direction that you are going. After your three turn, the right arm will help to check you by being directly behind you in the 6 o'clock position mentioned earlier. As you pull your arms in for jumps, use your back muscles and your hands to pull in, remembering to keep your shoulders down (figure 9.2a). You should feel your biceps, but the core strength should come from lifting your abdomen and pulling in with your lats.

In the air, use your right leg as the center of your in-air spin. Once you have initiated the turn, you should feel your body turn into your right leg so that your left ankle will cross briefly in front of your right as you would for a back scratch spin. Your left leg will go up and out for your landing as in the back scratch spin. Your arms should release before you land so that you can

c   d

(c) preparing to spring up, and (d) the spring, with the arm and leg moving to 9 o'clock.

a   b

Figure 9.2   *(a)* Tightening into the in-air position, and *(b)* landing position.

check them out. Keeping the arms slightly forward and the upper body over your hips will stabilize your landing. At the same time, your left leg will kick back in the low position we discussed earlier (figure 9.2b).

Doubles and Triples

Anyone who can do singles successfully will also be able to do doubles with a little bit of practice. Doubles require extra spring and speed. I often see skaters attempt to do doubles and triples and come to a screeching halt before they jump. You might be able to do a triple from a standstill, but you won't usually be able to get around if you are going too slow. Physics doesn't allow you to lift very high off the ice without speed (although I have had to learn to do this to perform on small ice). Thus, you need to practice doubles and triples with some speed. Of course, extra speed means that your preparation and the quickness with your arms and legs needs to increase. You need to have quick reflexes for a double or triple.

For both the double and triple you will do the same preparation and landing as the single. The difference occurs in how fast you pull into the back spin position. Your ability to get into this back spin position quickly is what turns a single into a double (figure 9.3). You must pull your body quickly into the back spin so that a slowed arm or leg does not deter your rotational speed in the air. For the double, you will prepare for your landing when you have overrotated the single.

The actual airtime for a triple is not that much different from that for a high single (figure 9.4). The only difference is how you use that time. Do you want a high, easy single, or a tight, fast triple? Quadruple jumpers use their airtime even more efficiently by pulling into their rotation immediately after takeoff. That is why quads are a blur in the air. For doubles and triples, you need to be strongly checked before and after the jump. Keep the right side slightly back before the jump and press the left side forward before you land.

Figure 9.3 For a double Salchow, get into the back spin position quicker than for a single.

Figure 9.4 A triple Salchow requires a very tight in-air position.

A common error that occurs with doubles and triples is trying to reach forward with the upper body to lift into the jump. Although this may make you feel as if you are giving greater muscle to the jump, you are actually taking your upper body too far away from your vertical axis. As a result, you will waste precious airtime as you work to be vertical in the air, and your jump will, most likely, be smaller. Bend into your knee, but work efficiently. Use your legs and your arms to give the jump spring and speed. If you use your shoulders and your hips, you will just build unnecessary muscle that will actually take away from the efficiency of working your body properly.

As you work on the Salchow, remember to use your arms and legs in the 6, 3, and 9 o'clock positions, checking to make sure that your upper body stays in place while you move your arms. Also remember to use both your legs, your skating edge, and foot to lift into the air so that you will be able to do high, easy Salchows. Although the jump may seem a bit more complicated than some of the others, if done correctly it will feel just as easy, and it will actually be fun!

10

Toe Loops

The toe loop is one of my favorite jumps and was one of the easiest for me to learn. In upcoming chapters, I will give you a few variations of this jump to try. In this chapter we will focus on the single, double, and triple, providing the proper technique to make the jump easy for you, too! As this is the first jump we will discuss that uses your toe to vault you into the air rather than your edge, I will also give you a few special techniques that will help you to spring into the air.

Singles

As with the Salchow, there are many ways to prepare for the toe loop. Most skaters begin with a forward left inside edge and do either a three turn or a mohawk to prepare for the jump. I often do toe jumps from footwork, so I usually do a three-turn entrance. If you do a three turn, it is very important that you work to check your hips after the turn. If you overrotate the three turn, your free leg may not be straight behind you, causing your toe in to be crooked.

If you begin with a right forward inside three turn, be sure to keep your right arm checked forward and your left arm directly behind you at about 6 o'clock. Then check the three turn with the left arm forward and the right arm directly behind at 6 o'clock. As you reach back with your left leg for the toe in, bend into your right leg and keep your upper body firm and lifted so that it stays in one line, like a pole (figure 10.1a). At the same time, use your left toe to vault from the ice. Think of the word *vault*. Many skaters think of

Figure 10.1   Single toe loop: *(a)* reaching back with the free leg, and *(b)* springing into

planting their left toe pick into the ice. If you think of vaulting, you will remember to toe in on the way up and use the toe pick to spring you into the air as opposed to planting you into the ice (figure 10.1b). Often I think of quick toe, so the pick goes in on the way up.

Toeing in on the way up will also prevent you from doing a toe Axel. Many skaters don't check their hips firmly before they jump. As a result, instead of toeing in when they are backward, they've already begun to turn. When you toe in, you should still be skating backward with your hips both facing forward over your toe instead of half turned forward. It looks as if you are doing a calf stretch. This will help you to really use your skating knee and foot to propel you into the air.

As you jump, your right leg will kick across your body (similar to the Salchow takeoff), and you will turn into your right leg for your back spin position. Your arms will once again come quickly to your chest with your elbows in tight. In the air, use your abdominal muscles to pull your body back in line. If you keep your body in the sharp diagonal line that you created from your head to your toe on the takeoff, you will be tipped in the air,

c   d

the air, (c) checking out of the turn, and (d) moving into landing.

making it difficult to land. On the landing, stop the rotation by opening your arms and landing with a low free leg (figure 10.1c and d).

Arms, as I have previously mentioned, are very important to jumps. To jump, you need to be very assertive with your arm placement. If you go into your jumps with a loose or nervous position with your arms, they will most likely not be in the correct position and your leg placement will be off. So you have to push your arms forward, reach, stretch, and scoop them into your body. I didn't skate with gloves on for many years for that reason. As a little kid, I got so used to wearing mittens that I skated with my hands in curled-up circles. They were very loose, and as a result I didn't have enough control. Especially when I began doing triples, I realized that I needed to use my hands for the jumps. My hands froze, but if they were too warm they would get lazy and I didn't use them for power. So remember to use your hands on all jumps. On the toe loop, keep them low and strong at waist level before you scoop them into your body—remembering, at the same time, to keep your shoulders down and to use your abdominal muscles to tighten and lift you into the air. Every little bit will help you get that extra spring and power.

Doubles and Triples

All of the same principles hold true for the double and triple toe loop. The only difference is that you will do everything *more*. You will need extra bend into your right knee, extra reach with your left foot, extra check with your left side, and greater quickness and speed in pulling into your rotational position. At the same time, use your abdominal muscles to pull into a vertical air position and your arms to scoop into the air and to help you to check the rotation on the way out. If you take the time to really work on your single toe, the double and triple shouldn't be too difficult. Compare the in-air tightness of the double and triple toe loops in figure 10.2.

As you work on toe loops, remember to use your check, arms, toe vault, and abdomen to scoop and lift you into the air. Although it may seem like a lot to think about right now, as you work on the jump the position will feel more natural. Before you know it you will be successfully landing singles, doubles, and eventually triples with ease and grace!

a   b

Figure 10.2 Compare the tightness of the in-air positions of *(a)* the double toe loop and *(b)* the triple toe loop.

11

Loops

While the toe loop has always been relatively natural for me, the loop felt like it took forever to learn. It probably didn't take that long, but it was a frustrating process, and for a while I hated to do it. In the loop, I eventually learned that I could not be aggressive. It is an edge jump, and as such it requires more finesse and less strength. As I got a little older I basically learned the triple loop, Lutz, and flip within a week of each other. So while the beginning stage of learning the single took forever, it did pay off because I was able to learn the doubles and triples with less difficulty. In this chapter, we will look at single, double, and triple loops. I hope that my early experiences with the loop will pay off a second time in that I will be able to pass along a few of my hard-earned tips.

Singles

The loop jump begins from a back edge. Your feet should be about hip distance apart before takeoff, with your right foot gliding on an outside edge and your left on an inside (figure 11.1a). Most skaters get into this preparation from back crossovers, but I liked to add a three turn before my preparation edge. It is not something you have to do; I just think it helped to calm me down. After your last crossover, step onto your right foot as if you would do one more crossover. Your feet should be hip- to shoulder-width apart so that your right hip is directly over your skate and slightly offset so that they are not directly side-by-side. If they are side by side, it probably means that you have squared off your hips before the jump and it will be harder for you to lift off the ice.

In this position, a lot of skaters center their weight evenly between their feet. I feel that my weight is on both feet, but I'm on my right leg. If your weight is centered between your legs, you will have to jump off your right hip, which means that you will end up pushing yourself over or lift off at an angle—risking injury through repetition. Think of keeping the left foot on the ice more for balance and guidance, to stay on the circle so that you will not jump sideways. As you bend your knees to lift off the ice, think of bending straight down so that your chest stays lifted and shoulders are now squared with the hips. This will allow you to stay over the edge (figure 11.1b). Your left leg will actually lift off the ice a split second before your right foot.

a   b   c

Figure 11.1 Single loop: *(a)* arm and leg position for the jump preparation, *(b)* edge tightening, and *(c)* tightening into rotational position after pushing up through the feet.

As you spring into the air, remember to jump through your feet to use the force of the edge (figure 11.1c). I had to be a little less aggressive with my arms on the loop than I was in the other jumps. My right arm was more to my side and my left was in front at 12 o'clock over my tracing. I felt them come from the side to scoop into my body so that I would ride the edge up. The jump should require less strength, instead feeling easy and light on the takeoff. In the air, your left leg will come into the back spin position with your wrists briefly crossed at your chest. Feel your chest and abdomen lift so that your body will come into line. On the landing, your left foot and arms will stop the rotation so that you will finish with your arms and legs in a stable and comfortable position.

Doubles and Triples

As I tried to work on double and triple loops, the hardest challenge for me was to relax. I had to almost think of not using my arms, because if I tried to make the jump big I would always have problems. I began the jump with my left arm directly in front of me, and then, as with the single, I would use it to come in and up. I almost didn't think of my arms. Instead, I focused on lifting my left knee into the jump. If I did anything besides that, I would jerk into the air, pulling my body off the circle, or I would bring my arms around too hard because I wanted to make the jump big. After trying all of the technical things that I could think of, I realized that I couldn't muscle a loop. It was an edge jump, so I had to be secure on the edge and ride it up.

For doubles you do all of the same things that you do in your single, except that you bend deeper into your right knee before the jump and use your muscle quickness to attain your rotational position faster. Remember that your weight should be on both feet until just before the takeoff when the left foot lifts up. Then use your right leg to spring off the ice. As you spring, keep your upper body lifted over the edge so that you don't fall into the circle. This may mean that you have to think of lifting your right side a little bit to maintain your center and balance as the edge increases before the takeoff. See figure 11.2 for a full double loop sequence.

The triple loop eventually became a very pretty jump for me. However, it was even harder to calm down for it. With all of the other jumps I have such a feeling for the definite technique that it felt as though in not doing enough I wouldn't successfully complete the jump or make it big enough. I had to do triples in a slow part of my program so that I could stay calm and just ride the edge up. I remember feeling as if they were so tiny when I didn't muscle them. Evy would shake his head and say, "Are you kidding? It was about a foot off the ice!" To me, it felt like an inch. As you work on triples (of course, after you have mastered the single and the double), remember that triples and quads require extra knee bend, a greater pulse before the takeoff, and a faster transition to your rotational position. You want to stay calm on the

a b c

d e

Figure 11.2 Double loop sequence (only one turn shown).

jump, but at the same time keep your abdomen and upper body lifted so that you will be able to use your reflexes on the takeoff and landing.

Some jumps may be harder than others for you to learn. For me, it was the loop. For you, it may be another jump. What I learned from my experience with loops is that after I had mastered the underlying technique, they seemed to get better the less I practiced them. If I practiced them too much, I would get too aggressive, and that went against what I needed to do. Occasionally you can be too aggressive on a jump and it will prevent your muscle memory from taking over. You need to put in the time to really learn the proper technique of a move. However, there may also be times when you need to give yourself a break. Doing so may help you to succeed with the move in the long run.

12

nlike the toe loop because you
jump with your opposite leg.
ut the timing and technique of
r in feeling to the Salchow. In
Salchow with a toe assist.
your toe to vault you into the
our arms and upper body. By
ou need to successfully land
hnique.

I
s
ju
ri
re
ar
ar
yo
yo

e three turn, just as in the
se be done, but before you
ur free leg (in this case your
three-turn jump entrance,
ple just step into the jump
l tightly into the air. If you
e to create the momentum
feel somewhat natural, so
the jump to lift off the ice.

For the flip, push into it with your right arm at twelve o'clock (directly in front of you). Your left arm should be at six (figure 12.1a). They will switch slightly on the turn, so that your left arm will be in front and your right arm in back after the turn. However, it will appear as if they did not move on the turn. After your three turn, your right side should be firmly checked back so that you are in control. From there, you will reach back with your free leg for the toe vault (figure 12.1b).

The feeling is almost the same as the Salchow. The only difference is that in the Salchow when you prepare to jump, your arms and legs go sideways and then scoop up. In the flip, your right arm is very important. It should be checked back in about a six o'clock position with your left arm at twelve. In this position, you should feel tension underneath your right shoulder blade. If you don't, it probably means that your shoulders are not pulled down or your arm is not in the correct position. Remember, if the shoulders are too high, when you scoop your arms in they will come in too high and you may throw yourself off balance. From here, you will feel your arms go down and then scoop up (figure 12.1c). I always think that it is better to feel your arms

a   b   c

Figure 12.1 Single flip: *(a)* pushing into the three turn, *(b)* checking the upper body, *(c)* the toe in for the lift

go down before they scoop up as opposed to just bringing them into your chest. You need the down to help lift you up. They should pull up into your body just below your chest in the air.

Just as in the toe loop, you will use your toe as a pole to vault you into the air. As you toe in, your free leg will pick straight behind you and you will feel that you toe in as you lift into the air. As you do this, bend into your left knee and remember to jump through your left foot, not just the knee, to give you a little extra lift into the air (figure 12.1d). In the air you will pull into your standard spin position. Your arms should be pulled in and your left leg should be crossed low and neat at your ankles (figure 12.1e). If you practiced this off the ice, you would feel your right foot reach back like a spring-loaded arrow. You would move your hips and upper body far enough back to your right foot so that the heel of your right foot could fully touch the ground. This is the same feeling you will have when you move your hips back to your foot in the air. In addition, you will feel your abdomen scoop in and back to your spine. Before you fully complete your revolutions, check out of the jump for the standard jump landing (figure 12.1f).

d   **e**   **f**

with arms scooping down, *(d)* spring into the air, *(e)* in-air position, and *(f)* landing.

Doubles and Triples

As with previous doubles and triples, the keys to turning singles into doubles are speed, using your arms, and using your toe to vault you into the air. If I pull my arms and legs in a little harder, I will do a double. If I pull in a lot, it's a triple. The reach of the free leg is also very important, but a big kick back is not necessary. You should feel your skating knee bend and the free leg should reach low behind you. It is especially important to remember on the flip, toe, and Lutz that you toe in on the way up. If you toe in and then jump, you don't have any impetus to jump. Your toe should help to lift you into the air.

For both the double and the triple, you will begin with the same entrance you used for the single. From there, remember to check your arms and use them to help scoop you into the air. It is even more important as you try multiple-revolution jumps that you are on balance before you spring into the air, so remember to really check your right side back after the three and use your arms and hands strongly to lift you into the air. Checking prevents the arms from rotating too early. Your arms should feel as if they are pulling through water to scoop down and up. At the same time, keep your shoulders low and your back and chest lifted with a firm abdomen.

Before you jump, bend more deeply into your front knee and use your free toe to vault you into the air. In the air, you will pull quickly into your rotational position (figure 12.2). As you land, you will need to check your arms forward and your leg back more firmly to help you stop the rotation. If you use your legs for the spring and your arms and legs for the rotation in the same way you have with your single and double, but with a bit more speed, you will more easily do triples.

Figure 12.2 Compare the in-air position of the single flip in figure 12.1e to that of the double flip shown here.

As with any jump, take your time with the flip and try to learn the technique properly under a coach's supervision. If you work to learn the proper technique, you will progress quickly and will not have to relearn the correct technique or eliminate bad habits.

13

Lutzes

The Lutz jump is similar to the toe loop and flip in that you use a toe assist. However, unlike the flip, the Lutz is done from a back outside edge. This is very difficult for skaters to do, and we often hear of people "flutzing" their Lutz. In a flutz, the skater drops to the inside edge just before takeoff on the Lutz, turning it into a flip. In this chapter, I will explain how to properly do a Lutz so that it is not a "flutz" and give you tips on landing the single, double, and triple Lutz.

Singles

The most common preparation for Lutz jumps is a series of back crossovers into the corner of the rink. As you work on the Lutz, you will probably want to begin your crossover preparation early, in order to gain enough speed to flow through the jump.

When working on doubles and triples, I realized that I needed more speed. This jump is all about timing. If you wait too long, you may have a harder time getting up into the air to rotate, and your timing will be off. Brian Boitano told me that he actually counts into his triple Lutz. He knows exactly what the timing should be for himself by count and he knows that if his preparation is too slow he's going to be too close to the boards. If his preparation is too fast, he will have trouble with the takeoff and landing of the jump. Timing in skating is everything.

As I prepare during my back crossovers, I like to do a right back outside edge that pulls me back to the side boards, giving me more room for the preparation for my back outside edge. Just before I prepare for the jump, I like to look back. I do this mainly for practical reasons. In the average practice session, often 20 people or more are on the ice at the same time. If you don't look, you could hit someone. You want to make it a quick movement, mostly moving your eyes (rather than your head) to look. After my back crossovers, I step on my right foot and do an outside change of edge to pull back to the boards as I look back over my left shoulder to check my pathway. I try to keep my right hand low in front of my navel so that I am in position to begin the jump preparation. It is OK to open your shoulders slightly to look if you can't turn your head enough, but you definitely want to keep your right hand low in front.

From the right back outside edge, I step onto my left foot with my right foot extended forward (figure 13.1). As I ride the left back outside edge, my right shoulder, more than in the other jumps, is at 6 o'clock. I move my arm from directly in front of me at 12 o'clock to pass close by my sides to 6, or even a little bit past to 7. Keeping it close is important because if you change your arms by bringing them around rather than through, it can make your upper body too loose. Although it is good to be relaxed, in this instance being too loose may make you less controlled, pulling you off the edge before the jump. So bring your arms straight down and then through on the change. Paul Wylie used to pass his arms around, but he really pressed his shoulders down. He had great Lutzes because he didn't let his shoulders get loose and he pressed his arms down so that they came around at waist level and kept them firm. I've explained to other skaters that they need to press their shoulders down as they position the right arm. When they try it they say, "Ouch! That cramps my shoulder blade!" My response is always, "That's great! Now you know that you're doing it right!" My right arm is almost like a rubber band. I feel it pull and pull and pull back and then

Figure 13.1 On the preparation for the Lutz, look back and keep the right hand low.

it snaps up into the air. It helps to give me the force I need to be able to get up into the jump.

At the same time that your arms change, your free foot (in this case the right) should pass close by your skating foot from the front to the back as you glide on the left back outside edge (figure 13.2). It will reach back as your hand goes down and through so that the arms and legs pass at the same time. You will feel the stretch with your free leg, as though someone is pulling it down and out. At the same time you will feel the twisting of the back through the right shoulder blade (figure 13.3). Then you will toe in and vault. The toe in happens on the way up, not during the bend down to create the vault. In the air, pull into your back scratch spin position with your arms and legs moving at the same

Figure 13.2 The free arm and leg pass close to the body before the reach back.

Figure 13.3 Reaching back with the free leg.

time into the low and neatly crossed position. In a single, you will prepare to land almost immediately after you jump because it doesn't require much rotation.

As I mentioned earlier, the most common error in the Lutz comes from rocking over on the blade before the jump. This actually turns the jump into a flip because you are on the inside edge, and judges are required to deduct for the mistake. The rules dictate that you do two of each jump, and one has to be in combination. So if you do two flips and two Lutzes, but your Lutzes are flips, you should be marked down. We still see people do flutzes at the Olympic level, which indicates how difficult this jump is, but it is a mistake, and you should work to land them correctly. When I was competing as an eligible skater, my coach Evy used to make Paul and me stay on the back edge for a full circle before we jumped so that we would learn to control the edge. It is important to realize and feel that your left foot is on an edge, and it should be on the outside when you toe in. Additionally, if you toe in too far to the inside of your left foot, it could cause you to go on the inside edge. As you toe in, feel that your right side is back and that your toe pick goes behind and almost past the tracing made by your left foot (figure 13.4). Your arm, as mentioned earlier, will be at almost 7 o'clock and your left hip will be underneath your body so that if you put your palm on your hip it would feel hollow, not sticking out. If you are that strongly checked and your free foot toes in past your skating foot, it is just about impossible for you to drop to the inside edge on the takeoff.

Figure 13.4 It is important for the left foot to stay on an outside edge for the toe in, with the right foot back.

Doubles and Triples

Someone asked me to do a single Lutz recently. It had been so long since I had done one that I really had to think about it. My body has become so accustomed to doubles and triples that in order to not do a double or a triple,

I couldn't pull my arms in and barely crossed my legs. They said, "Wow! How did you do that?" I was just trying not to turn. As I have mentioned in other chapters, how hard you pull in with your arms and how far you reach back with your free leg determines whether you do a single, double, or triple. Speed is also very important. We've all seen skaters go into jumps too slowly. They usually haven't given themselves enough time in the air to complete the rotation. Doubles and triples are all about timing. Of course you need some strength, but it is really timing that makes things happen. So for a double Lutz, you will skate with more speed into the jump, spring load your knee, and really use your arms and legs to pull into a tighter air position. Additionally, you need to feel a stronger commitment to the outside edge. A slight inside edge will set your shoulders off and will make it even more difficult to effectively pull in and land the jump. In all, you must do more in the same amount of time, so you must be very efficient in your movements.

A triple is just a single with two extra rotations. That doesn't sound so bad, does it? You already know what to do, so now you just need to speed up your air rotation, your speed into the jump, and your spring on the jump. Of course, it is extremely important that the single be just about perfect before you try doubles or triples because you are adding speed, spring, and rotation to the equation. So practice your singles, and even your doubles and triples, off the ice. When you practice off-ice, you are not practicing your takeoff, as that would be different on land, but rather you are getting accustomed to the in-air quickness and tightness. The wonderful thing about skating is that we can always jump higher, spin longer or faster, or skate with more speed. Continue to work on making yourself a better skater because the thrill of doing something better the next day will always be there.

Axels

The Axel jump usually takes a long time for skaters to learn. I don't remember how long it took me to learn it, but I do remember that my coach would not allow me to compete or have a program with music until I could do a solid Axel. The Axel can seem scary because you are looking in the direction that you jump before you take off, and you can trip on your toe pick. It is also a half revolution more than other jumps, so you need to find your pulled-in rotational position faster than with other jumps. However, the good news is that it incorporates a lot of the same principles that we have already discussed in previous chapters. While it is a bit more challenging, a good single, double, or triple Axel is not impossible.

Singles

Axels are done from a forward outside edge, and, unlike other singles, a single Axel is actually one and a half revolutions, so that the landing is backward. Skaters often use the waltz jump as a preparation for the Axel because the waltz jump takeoff is also from a forward outside edge. I still do the waltz jump to help me warm up for Axels. However, in a waltz jump you are much more open in the air (figure 14.1). In the Axel, you keep your hips squared off and pass the free knee close by the skating leg. As you begin to work on your Axel, it is OK to do the waltz jump, but use it mainly for the

Figure 14.1   The waltz jump's in-air position is very open.

preparation back edge and forward outside takeoff, not as a preparation for the in-air feeling of the Axel.

Most skaters prepare for the Axel by doing back crossovers counterclockwise, with the left foot crossing over the right. The Axel is tricky because you must be on a solid back outside edge before you step forward and into the jump. As you do your last back crossover, rotate your upper body so that your right foot is on a strong outside edge (figure 14.2a). A common mistake that skaters make on the back outside edge is that they don't turn, and thus they stay facing forward on the back outside edge. This opens their shoulders and blocks the upper body for the forward edge. As you ride the back outside edge, keep your shoulders and hips square as you look in the direction you are moving (figure 14.2b). If your arms are behind you before the jump, you will block yourself for the timing of the jump and pull yourself off the circle (the edge). You should feel that you are on such a solid edge that you could jump at any time. Whether it's a waltz jump, double Axel, or triple, it is the easiest and most consistent if you stay square on the edge and then step forward comfortably for the jump.

The step-forward edge placement is very important. From the back outside edge, you will bring your arms back and step forward on the left forward outside edge (figure 14.3). When you step, you will step slightly off the circle so that you are on a new circle—not the circle you were on in the back edge. Stepping on the same circle can cause a number of problems. So step out so that your left foot will be at almost a 120-degree angle to your

a   b

Figure 14.2 In preparation for the Axel, *(a)* the right foot is on a strong outside edge, and *(b)* the back rotates as you stay on the outside in preparation to step forward.

right foot. If you are on a circle that rounds to the boards, you would feel that you step out toward the boards.

As you step forward and bend into your left knee, your arms will swing down by your sides and go behind you, with straight elbows. Many skaters bend their elbows as they prepare to jump. Actually, that is not a good idea because there isn't enough tension in the arms to help lift the body into the air. You should feel that your arms are straight, but not locked (figure 14.4). Going into the Axel, I feel tension and pressure

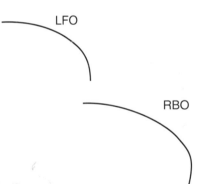

Figure 14.3 Proper edge placement for the back-to-forward transition in preparation for the Axel.

just below my elbow in the forearm. The arms will come to the front on the back outside edge and then, elbows straight, they will come back and through with the free leg (figure 14.5).

You'll notice that some skaters don't use their arms when doing triples. I bring them back, then through to scoop up, giving myself more height. However, you will probably figure out a rhythm that feels most comfortable

Figure 14.4 Stepping forward with the arms coming down, elbows straight but not locked.

Figure 14.5 The arms and free leg coming through together.

for your arms as you work on the Axel. If you keep your movements fairly simple and give yourself only a few things or even one thing to think of, there is less confusion and, often, fewer mistakes.

As you jump, your right knee will come through close by the skating leg so that you jump straight up. You want to use your free leg and your arms to give the jump lift. Thinking *through* with the free leg will help keep you on a straight axis in the air. When you bring the leg through and up, you want to rotate at the top of the lift (not on the way up). It is as if you step up onto a stair and the rotation happens on the stair. This way you have time to check out for the landing.

As you lift into the air, remember to jump all the way through your left foot. As you do this, you will skid slightly off your left edge (figure 14.6). This is one of the few times in skating that a scraped edge is a good thing! Many skaters try to keep a clean edge on the Axel. That may seem like a good idea, but it actually gives you less height on the jump and less control. It's much easier if you skid a little on the left edge because you can use the ice to help spring you into the air.

In the air, your free knee will straighten as you turn into your back spin rotation position. At the same time, scoop your arms in and lift up from your abdomen. By the end of the first half of your rotation, you should have your left leg crossed low over your right. As you rotate, prepare for your landing by uncrossing the feet and pulling the leg back into a standard landing position.

Doubles and Triples

It may sound a bit simplistic, but a double Axel is really only one more revolution than a single. Remember, for doubles and triples you need extra speed, extra knee bend for your spring, and a tighter air position (figure 14.7). I found that one additional ingredient was

Figure 14.6   Lifting off the left foot.

necessary on the double Axel. When I was first learning it, I couldn't quite land it. Karen Magnussen, the 1973 world champion, was watching me one day and she told me to breathe in on the way up. She said to actually make the "huh" breath sound. I did it, and boom! I landed the double Axel the first time I tried it. If you breathe in when you are jumping, your body tends to straighten. You don't usually breathe in and then lean sideways. So, just breathing in from under the ribs made me straight and maybe gave the extra half-inch I needed to land the jump. I've told this to other people, and it works. This trick also works for toe jumps and for triple–triple combinations. Your breath becomes the spring to help vault you back into the air the second time. I have gotten to the point where I don't have to make the noise, but it did teach me to keep strong and centered in my core. Perhaps it's just letting the body work the way it needs to without thinking about all of the details. As I've said over and over, as you work on all of your skating moves, focus on one thing. If it's the right thing, you will easily do the move because proper technique will happen without your having to focus on all of the details.

Figure 14.7   Double Axel sequence (one rotation shown).

A triple Axel requires greater speed and dexterity than a double, but it is not unattainable. I practiced the triple Axel one week of the year and I could do them, but I never worked on them for competition. At the time, it was more important to my coaches and me that I work to become a well-rounded skater. If I only focused on one jump in competition, I could have blown the entire program if I missed it. So I used the triple Axel as something to try out and play around with. I think that if I had continued to work on them I would have risked injury. The reasons are simple: you have to go a little higher, spin a little faster, and come down a little harder. It is very hard on your body, and we have seen ankle and knee injuries in most of the women who have tried them.

I have always enjoyed men's skating, and have worked to stay on par with the men in my jumping ability. Physically, on average, men are able to handle triple Axels and quads more easily than women. Women are continuing to push harder physically, and it is possible for more women to do triple Axels. However, anyone who works on the triple Axel should do so safely and should not stress their bodies to land the jump.

Above all else, try to work your muscles in an efficient way. They should not be loose, but they should also not be so tight that you can't move them.

When champion athletes win races, competitions, or tournaments, inevitably they say that on that day they felt incredibly relaxed. While it may seem odd that a person who can run the mile in record time can be relaxed, there is great simplicity to the statement. If your body is relaxed, it is able to work effectively, without harm or distraction from unnecessary motion. Although I am not advising that you work without tension in your muscles or speed in your movements, it is important, especially on a jump like the triple Axel, to know why you are moving a body part and to make your movements have purpose.

15

Jump Combinations and Variations

Now that we have worked on all of the hard stuff, it's time to use those skills in combinations and learn a few jumps you may not often see in competition. In this chapter we will discuss jump variations, such as the delay, the stag jump, the split, and the Russian split. In addition, we will learn specific tips for doing jumps in combination. Combinations and variations may seem more difficult, but remember that skating is all about timing. A variation may be as simple as changing the ending or slowing down your timing in the air, and you may find that in practicing combinations and variations, your single jumps improve.

Combinations

Two types of jump combinations may be done: jumps that have a step down between them, and jumps that don't. In a jump combination, turns or connecting steps between the jumps are not allowed. If a skater turns or performs a connecting step (such as a three turn or a mohawk between the jumps), the combination is called a jump sequence, and this is not the same as a jump combination.

I first began doing jump combinations at a very young age. I didn't watch a lot of skating on TV then. I had brothers and I was the youngest, so we usually watched hockey. When I did watch skating, I watched the men because they did the more difficult, exciting jumps. I liked strong, aggressive skating, and though the girls could be strong and aggressive, they didn't do any of the tricks, or so I thought. I remember watching Mark Cockerell in the 1984 Olympics do a triple toe–triple toe combination. I decided that I not only wanted to do it but that I also *could* do it. Within a week, I landed my first triple toe–triple toe combination. I was 15 years old and competed at the novice level. In 1985, I competed at Eastern championships in Lake Placid. I had missed my first attempt at the combination in my long program, though I had been doing it in practice. I was in the middle of my program and I looked at my coach and asked, "Should I?" She said, "Yes!" At the end of my program I did a triple–triple combination. We didn't have a short program then, and after figures I had been in last place. In my free skate, I skated first and received first place, to receive the silver medal overall. I tell this story not because I want you to think more of me, but because it does prove that anything is possible if you believe in yourself. I think it is also important because triple–triple combinations and combinations in general seem tricky. However, just as with anything else, a few basic principles apply; and if you execute the skills correctly, you can accomplish the combinations with ease.

In combinations you want to purposely keep the first jump smaller so that you have the flow to do the second one. The second jump should be bigger than the first, so you need to land the first jump in preparation for the next one. You shouldn't rush the landing and jump too fast into the next one or rotate before you leave the ice. After the first jump, use your knee bend, arms, and breath to spring back into the air. Your skating knee is like a machine—you use it to go down and up. Remember, to get up, you have to first go down. So land the first jump then bend for the next lift up.

Taking a deep breath in before you jump into the second jump is also very important. Your breath will help to release tension and will also help to lift you straight back up into the air.

Checking after the first jump is extremely important. You need the same elastic feeling in your arms and legs that you worked to create in your first jump. After the first jump, really check so that you can use the momentum of the first jump to take you straight up into the air again. Since you may be jumping on the second jump from less speed, you need to make the first jump low and quick so that the second jump has flow into it and can be bigger than the first. This also makes the combo more exciting. If, for example, you were working on a Lutz–loop, you would land the Lutz with your free foot (left) in front in preparation for the loop so that you could bend into your skating leg and lift straight back up (figure 15.1).

As you work on combination jumps, keep in mind that they don't have to be done with the harder jump first. For example, I didn't like the loop as much because I needed to be very calm and less aggressive for the jump. When I had to do combination jumps in the technical program, the rules would sometimes say to do a loop combination. I would do a double loop–triple toe. Everyone thought that it was harder, but for me it was much easier. If I had done a double after the toe, it would have been much harder because I needed to relax to do the loop, and a combination requires you to be assertive as you lift into the second jump. You may find that certain combinations work better for you, too, so play around and see what feels the most natural.

Figure 15.1   In a Lutz–loop combination, the Lutz is landed with the free foot in front.

Jump Variations

Like spin variations, jump variations are limited only by your imagination. Years ago, every turn had a jump to accompany it. There were rocker jumps and counter jumps. Modern skaters have replaced the older jumps with faster, higher, and bigger jumps, but a true jump variation may be as simple as changing your timing in the air, your takeoff, or your landing to transform a basic jump into something unusual.

Delayed Jumps

My favorite delay jump has always been the delayed double flip. I like how it feels because it just flies. Everyone loves to do doubles and triples because they are fun and you feel great accomplishment. However, a delayed jump can soar and have greater impact if done correctly. I was actually taught to do all of my jumps with delays so that I would learn to get the height that I needed for triple jumps, and to get the quick turn needed to get around in time for the landing (which also helped with the tight in-air position). It's

Figure 15.2   Toe jump delay in the air (hanging time).

a very good exercise. The problem was that I tried to make them really big and open them as long as I could, so I would sometimes fall on a relatively easy jump, looking for the delay. Keep in mind that you do have to come down at some point. However, it is worth going for it and seeing how long you can delay so that you will continue to push and expand your capabilities.

You can practice delays standing on the ground or on the ice. I would turn away from the boards so that the glass was behind me and stand with my left arm in front and my right arm straight behind. As we've discussed earlier, a lot of people go into jumps with their arms at about 3 or 4 o'clock, which doesn't give them the strength and aggressive feeling they need to jump. Remember to keep your arms at 12 and 6. As I practiced, I would jump and bring my arms straight down by my sides, and then, when I was 180 degrees, looking at the glass, I would bring them straight out to my sides before pulling in tight. For a split second, I would be able to see my reflection in the glass with my arms straight out at my sides before I pulled in (figure 15.2). If you practice delaying your jumps, even if they are singles or doubles, you will be able to jump higher. And, if you are doing singles or doubles, there is no reason they shouldn't be great!

Splits and Stags

Both the stag and split jumps may be done from a regular flip jump preparation or a mohawk. You will do a half rotation in the air, using your left leg to touch down, and push onto your right leg on the landing. In your stag, your front leg should be bent at the knee and your back leg should be lifted and stretched behind you (figure 15.3). You should look as if you were doing splits with your front leg bent, and should have a stretched out line from knee to opposite ankle. You can do a variation with both legs bent. In the splits, both legs will be stretched so that your legs are parallel to the ground (figure 15.4).

In both the stag and the split, your arms are usually stretched to your sides. Do not detract from the hard work you are doing to create your split by lifting your shoulders. If your arms are too high, the position does not look controlled and your neck is lost, unless you make sure your shoulders stay down. Feel your back muscles, not your biceps, holding your arms in the air so that you will have a nice elongated position from your back to your head.

Figure 15.3 Stag.

A variation of the split jump is the Russian split. Russian split jumps are often executed two or three in a row and placed on a circular pattern. When done well, it is exciting, but if

© J. Barry Mittan

Figure 15.4 Paul Wylie's split.

the second split is not as strong as the first you can lose the energy of the crowd. I don't often do two in a row because the second is not always as strong. Keep in mind that you have only a few minutes on the ice in a performance to show your best skills, so do jumps and moves that you can do comfortably.

For the Russian split, use your left toe pick to spring into the ice. In the air, your legs will be stretched wide at your sides as if you were sitting on the ground with your legs open in a wide V. Try to feel your legs above your hips to get the maximum stretch. In the air, reach for your toes. As in the regular split, your back should be stretched, your head lifted, and your shoulders in place—not up at your ears.

Russian splits can also be done from flip or Lutz takeoffs. In the air you can split earlier so that you can turn into your rotational position on the second half of the jump. This becomes a split flip and is a fun variation to learn. Paul Wylie does split flips wonderfully.

More Variations

Variations may be as simple as changing the ending of the jump. I used to like to do a big Axel or a double Axel with a back spiral (with a bent knee) on the landing. It looked as though I landed directly in the spiral position because it happened so fast, but I actually landed the jump first and then lifted the free leg higher to make the spiral happen.

As you work on your jumps, keep your arms low. Sometimes you will realize in a performance or practice that the first jump was strong and you want to add a combination. If your arms are low, you can check and jump instead of just landing. However, if you know that you definitely plan to do only one jump, it is also fun to experiment with landing with your arms higher or in a position that suits your music. It is just another variation that will give your skating style and individuality.

Other variations include the tuck Axel and the Walley. For the tuck Axel you tuck your knees up to your chest after you spring as you rotate. You can tuck with your knees together or with your ankles crossed. For the Walley, you use your edges to build momentum for the jump. As you jump, push your free foot behind you and jump your standing foot to your free foot so that they touch in the air (figure 15.5).

Many skaters have created their own signature variations. Brian Boitano, for example, created the 'Tano Lutz. It is the same as a regular Lutz, but Brian increased the difficulty by raising his arm over his head. He makes it look easy, but it actually requires a great deal of upper-body strength. In changing the arm position, he has made the jump look completely different and more exciting.

The back flip is also a jump variation. This jump is used in shows because it is illegal in eligible skating competitions. I advise most competitors not to worry about back flips right now. They can be dangerous if they are not

Figure 15.5 Walley sequence.

learned correctly and are not necessary to your development as a skater. I mention it here only to remind you that jump possibilities are limitless. Years ago, skaters did rocker jumps and counter jumps; now Surya Bonaly does one-foot back flips, and quads are a staple of men's skating—a constant reminder that the athletic and technical bar will continue to be raised.

Part 4

Skating With a Partner

You may have already begun skating with a partner. If you have not, now is your chance! In this section I will discuss skating with one partner, as in pairs or dance, or with many partners, as in synchronized skating.

If you already have a partner or team or are looking for one, you may have envisioned your ideal partner. While skating with someone else can be a fun and rewarding experience, a variety of problems can arise. Before we launch into the next chapters, I would like to discuss ways to find partners or teams, ways to improve your partnerships, and ways to keep your team together.

Exercising creativity and working well together make partner skating an enjoyable and rewarding experience.

Finding a Partner

Fred Astaire seemed to always have an array of eligible partners, but in the skating world finding a partner is a little like finding a needle in a haystack. For me, the process was unusually easy. I began skating with my coach's little brother, Bobby Martin. We had known each other for almost ten years before we began, so we felt fairly comfortable with one another. In some circumstances, there may be an eligible partner in your own rink who matches you physically, technically, and personally. However, for many skaters, this is not the case. They must work to find a partner.

There are a few good ways to look for partners. In the last few years, the USFSA and PSA have made concerted efforts to match pairs and dancers. Both maintain databases that can be helpful for matching partners. In addition, the USFSA sponsors camps for pairs and dancers who both have and are looking for partners. I remember going to a pairs camp with Bobby for two weeks in Lake Placid. For that two-week period, I was able to work with many of the top pairs coaches in the country, such as Ron Ludington and Kerry Leitch.

As you begin your search, the first step is to think about the kind of partner you would like. Are you looking for a regular partner to take lessons with, someone to train a few hours a week with, or a serious competitive partner? Think about your goals. Do you want to pass all of your tests? Compete nationally or internationally? Perform in shows? Also consider your training style. How many days a week do you like to practice? How many hours a day? Do you prefer to work with one coach or a team? Some other considerations may include the following.

- Are you willing to relocate for a partner?
- Are you and your partner willing to relocate to work with a specific coach?
- How much money are you willing to spend on training?

Talk to a lot of people. Find out what other skaters at your level are committing to in terms of time, effort, and payment, and be realistic about what you want and are looking for in another person. Look for someone who is at your level. Many people try to skate with partners who are several levels above them. There are some situations where a large level difference will work out, but for the most part this can cause unnecessary tension in a partnership.

Once you have an idea of what you are looking for, skate with as many people as possible to become familiar with different styles. You may wish to attend sessions at your rink or other rinks that you do not normally attend both to let people see you skate and to let others know that you are looking.

In addition, if you are interested in skating with people outside of your area, you should prepare a resume. Your resume should include your basic stats, such as contact information, height, weight, and coaches you regularly work with, as well as your skills and accomplishments. It is also helpful to include a headshot and a full body picture with your resume to help the potential partner determine the physical match. You may also need to put together a video. The video should include your most recent skating, such as your program if you are a freestylist, or dances at your level. If possible, skate with someone else on the tape so that potential partners may see how you look skating with a partner.

As you begin to send out resumes and seek tryouts, work on the skills that you will need in order to compete at your level for the upcoming season. Also work on your basic skating skills such as stroking, as you will most definitely look for a match in leg lines and extension with your partner.

On tryouts, above all be courteous, show up on time, and be prepared. Very rarely does the match feel perfect immediately. You are looking to see whether there is potential and whether this is the kind of partner and situation that you would like. Pay attention to the physical match in the tryout, but don't make that the only deciding factor. If you are muscular and your potential partner is very thin, the look may be wrong. However, you can skate with someone who you look perfect with, but if you do not share common goals and have difficulty communicating, the partnership will always be a struggle. Also pay attention to life off the ice. You will spend a great deal of time training, in most cases, but if you are moving to a new partner, you also need to know that life off the ice will be great too. While getting a partner may seem like half the battle, the real work has only just begun!

The Partnership

People say that skating with a partner is like a marriage, but it's not. I don't see my husband all day long. We do things at night or in the morning or on the weekends, but in a marriage you are not ordinarily with your spouse all day long every day. In a partnership, you are always touching and you have to be really comfortable with each other. You both have invested time and money to be able to skate with each other. Thus, it's really important that you and your partner get along, not only to make your partnership successful but also to make it fun. The following list should serve as a stepping-stone to keep your partnerships happy, successful, and long lasting.

1. **Make partnership commitments and goals season by season.** Think about your one-week, one-month, yearly, and long-term goals and write them down so that you both agree on what you are working toward. Then make the commitment to try to reach those goals one year or one season at a time. If you will be competing and have moved to train together, this time frame allows you to make school, living, and work commitments. At the end of the season, reevaluate.

2. **Agree to costs and time.** Although this may have been discussed before you became partners, it's vital to clarify the issue once you are skating together. What worked in theory may or may not work in practice.

3. **Find coaches who work for you as a team.** Find coaches you are both comfortable with. Try to get both a man and a woman as advisers, particularly in pairs or dance, because each coach will intrinsically understand the male and female roles.

4. **Manage your time together.** Skating is a very expensive sport. When you are on the ice, it is time to skate. If you and your partner have things to discuss, you should meet before or after the session so that your time on the ice is used most efficiently.

5. **Respect each other.** All too often partners experience an adversarial, finger-pointing relationship with each one trying to prove his or her worth. This is often the result of two people who do not have complete knowledge of the required techniques training together. In some cases, partners were trained in different styles and techniques and are constantly challenged by the other person's idea of what's "right." Keep in mind that both members of a partnership or all members of a team bring their own skills and assets to the team and that the team could not exist without its members. Work through the tougher times by listening to each other, and you will move beyond them.

6. **Make compromises.** When one partner becomes completely set in his or her ways, the person and the partnership stop growing and learning. Recognize that you need to work together, and through creative thinking you will usually find ways to meet in the middle.

7. **Learn from each other.** Instead of blaming each other for past errors, talk about what you would like to fix the next time. This will move your work forward positively. Also, pay attention to corrections given to your partner, as they may apply to you at a later time, or you may be able to help your partner with the correction.

8. **Keep it interesting.** Your workouts will get boring quickly if you do the same things every time you skate. Very simple changes like different warm-up music, or little games like seeing who can express the most, or working specifically on knee bend or jumps or edges that day, can add variety. This will also establish daily goals that will give you a sense of accomplishment and keep your work fun.

9. **Recognize that results come in all forms.** Partnerships take time to gel. If you look at any of the champions today, you will find that in most cases they have skated a long time together. They didn't usually win the first year. If you and your partner have been together several years and are not producing results, it may be time to think about your approach. However, results may not be found in a first place, but in good practices, improved technique and artistry, increased unison, or any variety of successes.

10. **Communicate! Communicate! Communicate!** You may wish to schedule weekly or monthly meetings away from the rink to check in with each other and talk about your progress. Respect what you have and communicate with each other to make your team strong. Keep in mind that you can also communicate without speaking. Whether it's synchronized skating, pairs, or dance, you always need to be aware of each other and look at each other.

Throughout your career you will see skaters stop skating because they've lost a partner. Sometimes things don't work, no matter how hard you've tried. Don't let a partner determine your love of skating. When you skate regularly with one person, you come to rely on that person in ways that you don't realize. If you relearn to skate alone, or never stop, you will not only have the knowledge you gained from skating with a partner, but will also be an improved solo skater. Skating is a challenging but rewarding process and you never know what new successes or partnerships await!

16

Ice Dancing

I've always thought that ice dancing was harder than pairs. A one-arm Detroiter or a throw Axel is not that different from skating singles, but to skate side by side with someone in a tight dance hold always caused me to wind up on my knees, or worse! If you look at old-fashioned skating pictures, before people jumped, they were on the ice, dancing, often wearing coats and muffs as they skated together. Today, ice dancing is a bit different. Like great actors and actresses, ice dancers play a variety of roles. To be a great ice dancer, you must have solid skating skills and be willing to stretch your body and imagination to dance in different ways. The compulsory dances have variations of waltzes, foxtrots, tangos, and cha-chas. Each compulsory dance requires that you learn different skills to improve your overall skating. They also give you the opportunity to try various rhythms to experience the expressive drama that is part of each dance. These skills are taken to the exciting original and free dances.

In the previous section we discussed finding a partner and keeping your partnerships together. However, to be a great partner you also need to be a great solo dancer. In this section, we will discuss some basic dance concepts, providing skills that will help you present each dance. A few ice dancing coaches have assisted with this chapter, including Collin Sullivan, a former national and international senior dance competitor and coach. Although ice dancing may seem difficult, remember as you work that the best skaters and dancers move with efficiency and style, and they never stop trying to improve.

Elizabeth Punsalan and Jerod Swallow embody the modern ice dance team with their solid skating skills and creative choreography.

Ice Dancing Concepts

To be a great dancer, you must have proper body positions. Strong basic technique will help you to achieve stretch in your positions and enable you to skate on deep edges with speed, alone and with a partner. All of the skills that we discussed in chapter 1—skating with speed, good posture, using your edges and lobes, skating with rhythm, and being able to perform all of your turns easily—become even more important when you skate with someone else. Each of these skills must be worked on with additional conscientiousness, using your hips, knees, and ankles to keep your lower body soft as your upper body stretches into lines.

You may have heard dancers say that a certain skater has "soft knees." What this means is that the skater uses the knees to cushion strokes. We use our knees to keep our legs and hips soft and pliable so that we will best be able to move. With this added freedom of movement, we are able to skate faster. The moment any coach tells a group of skaters to "skate faster," you will see the group scurry, shoulders forward, rears released, pushing from the balls of their feet. While they may gain some speed, they will have worked harder than necessary. Think of speed like pulling back a rubber band to release a water balloon. The farther you pull back, the farther the balloon will carry. Skating through proper alignment with our ankles, hips, shoulders, and ears in line between strokes, we use our knees to load up energy. The faster we can get back down into them, the more speed and flow we will have on the next stroke. You can check this by stopping on any transition in basic stroking. You should always be on balance with your knees bent and your feet flat in your skates so that you are neither too far forward nor too far backward on the blade (figure 16.1).

In using our lower bodies and backs to initiate movement, we have greater freedom in what we do with our upper bodies. If you take a deep breath, you will feel the muscles just under your shoulder blades and on the sides at the widest part of your back expand. It is this meaty muscle—the latissimus dorsi (lats)—that is responsible for keeping your upper body lifted.

Once your body mechanics are strong, you can work on improving your body line and stretch. Dancers take basic skating shapes and magnify them, stretching from every muscle to create movement to music. While all skaters work in these ways, dancers work on lengthening lines to create interesting shapes. There are, of course, specific errors that can occur, but if you start by strengthening your basic skating technique, you will have a solid base from which to create stretch and line.

Partnering

While you do need to be a strong individual skater, in ice dancing you also need to know how to skate with another person. Partnering involves a few special skills. These include *taking hold, tracking, unison,* and *timing.*

Holds

Taking hold begins the conversation of your dance. Holds are a basis for connection and are used in compulsory dances, original dances, and free dances for choreographic purposes. Whether you are skating with the same partner you have had for years or are with someone for the first time, the way you take hold tells a lot about how effective you will be as a dancer and can also tell others how connected you and your partner are to each other.

Taking dance hold on the ice is very similar to taking hold on the dance floor. My dad always taught me that it is best for the man to have an open hand so that the lady is able to put her hand in his with room to maneuver. If you and your partner are too tight in your hold, or if the man affectionately squeezes the woman's hand, you both may feel stuck or as if you were being pulled off your feet. You need a little space so that you can fix what you are doing on the dance floor, and in skating, too.

a

b

Figure 16.1 Both knees should be slightly bent during *(a)* the transition to *(b)* the next stroke.

To effectively take hold, first remember that the hold should not be used as a way to steady each other. You should each be skating easily on your own, holding each other lightly. If you are skating in an open position, hand in hand, both partners should skate with their elbows in a soft position, not overextended or locked.

Your arms should always be in front of your body. If your arms are behind your body, your chest will most likely be too far forward and your body will be out of alignment. If your elbows are in front of you, your back will be in the proper alignment and you will have the best control over your position because you will be able to use your back and abdominal muscles for balance and control.

Though your hold should not be too tight, neither should it be too loose. In a position like the traditional waltz hold, the woman's hand is pressing just beneath the man's clavicle while the man is gently using the palm of his hand underneath her shoulder blade to keep her close (figure 16.2). It is especially important for the man to remember not to hold the woman too high on her back in this hold. It will make both skaters too close in the top and too far away in the hips and will ruin the give-and-take that is needed in the hold. The pressure of the woman gently pushing away and the man holding her in keeps the upper bodies apart. Your hands should be between your bodies so that you have equal pressure between you. In a hold like the waltz, you especially want to have a wide base with your feet so that you have room to skate, and your top line (the line that your shoulders and arms create in hold) is uninterrupted.

Finally, in all holds, both skaters should be somewhat relaxed and comfortable. Remember that tension is the antecedent of true movement. In some dances, such as just before the rocker in the foxtrot, it is acceptable, and even

Figure 16.2 The traditional waltz hold.

Figure 16.3 The foxtrot hold.

advisable, for the woman to slide her left hand to the man's back so that her left palm is cupping the man's right shoulder blade. It is also a good idea for the couples to be slightly offset with their sternums facing each other in this position (figure 16.3). This will give you both room to move in a relaxed and efficient manner.

Tracking

Tracking is how you lead and follow your partner; it relates to how you and your partner's feet and bodies are aligned. Each dance, hold, and element will determine how you track your partner. In some dances, you will be skating directly at your partner with your knees slightly offset so that your foot will skate between your partner's feet. In other dances, you may skate completely side by side or partially outside your partner. In most cases, as with the compulsories, the dance and hold will dictate how you should track your partner. However, if you are working on choreography, you may need to discuss and resolve tracking issues together so that you can both comfortably skate without fear of tripping each other.

One of the most common problems that occurs with tracking is that each skater tries to skate too far away from the other in an attempt to have more space. However, as you and your partner are attached in dance hold, generally, the farther away from each other you skate, the more difficult it is for you to skate comfortably together. If you are feeling uncomfortable, talk to your partner or stop in the middle of the element and look down to see how closely you are skating. You will often find that there is plenty of room for both of you to feel comfortable in the position. You may also find that one of you needs to alter edge depth or upper-body hold so that you can both skate to your full potential. One general rule to keep in mind is that the person skating backward will set the lobe for the person skating forward to track and follow.

We often hear people say that there is *lead* and *follow* in tracking. However, this does not mean that the man always leads and the woman always follows. And following is not always a passive action. There may even be times when both skaters lead. Although one partner may more aggressively lead at times, it does not mean that the other partner should back down. You should both continue to strongly skate your roles.

Unison

Whether you have a regular partner or are working with someone only for testing, you must think about *unison*. We may notice a team that just seems to look "together," though we are not sure why. Often, it is because the timing of their movements is unified. However, unison relates not only to timing, but also the height and turnout of the free leg, arm position, and placement of the heads and bodies. As with every skill in skating, unison is something that has to be practiced to be executed well. It usually takes time to learn how to synchronize your movements with your partner's as you need to understand the partner's internal rhythm and style of skating. Working off the ice with mirrors or having someone watch you skate to help you determine whether things are matching are the best ways to practice this. It may also be helpful to have your skating videotaped so that you and your partner can check for your unison. If you are not matching, you may have to make compromises so that, for example, one person tilts the head slightly more in and the other agrees to tilt slightly more out until a match is achieved.

There are times that you may not want to match. Other times, for choreographic purposes, you may want to be exact mirror images. Whatever the case may be, make sure that both skaters agree whether the movement should be unified and work on it together to make the best artistic picture.

Timing

Timing relates to when you do a move to the music and your internal timing and rhythm together. For example, on free dance moves like drapes and assisted jumps, you must set a rhythm for each move, knowing by count when the drape or takeoff for the lift will occur. Although compulsory dances have strict tempo, skaters have long been known to stretch the musical limits. As artists play with their mediums, dancers tempt their music, working to be in control of their movements and timing. They may hold a stretched position a little longer, borrowing from the music to increase an extension and then speeding their movements out of it to stay on time. As you work on this skill, stay in line with the rules, and try to make decisions as a team about how you will hold your extensions or the quickness or slowness of your movements. This will unify your timing and add variety and creativity to your choreography.

Setting the Mood

In recent years, there has been a movement to remove compulsories from the test structure. If you watch compulsories at a competition, the same music is played over and over again and the same steps are skated. An uneducated

Effective artistic expression conveys the story and tone of the dance and music.

watcher may think that they are boring, giving ice dancing a bad reputation. However, compulsory dances are actually very important because they teach skaters to use their edges, skate with a partner and alone, and move to a variety of tempos. The skills used in compulsories to accurately portray the feeling of each dance are later used in original dances and free dances, giving skaters a basic skill and acting level.

Keep in mind that in all areas of competition, the sport was initially about dancing. To that end, you should learn about the different styles of dance. How were they done? Who did them and where? Is there a typical style of movement or dress that they are affiliated with? Many skaters make the mistake of thinking that tangos and waltzes were first done on the ice. If they studied the history of the dances, they could more accurately and truthfully portray the necessary emotions and artistic expression. Each dance has a varied lineage and history. In examining just five dances, we can see how distinct each style is.

WALTZ. Soft, flowing movements characterize the waltz. The dance portrays romance, so partners should look at each other. The woman should feel like the queen of the ball, while the man is her Prince Charming.

PASO DOBLE. The Paso Doble is the dance of the matador in a bullfight. The waltz may be the woman's chance to shine, but the Paso is the man's dance. He should skate with a strong machismo and toned positions. However, the woman should not be outdone. She can think of her role in three different ways: as the cape, as a flirty flamenco dancer, and as the bull. She may take all of these roles at varying times throughout the dance. Movements should be sharp, with intricate footwork and strong lines to match the music. You may express by challenging each other with long, fiery looks.

QUICKSTEP. The quickstep is directly derived from ballroom. A light, skipping knee action should be used throughout. The partners should exude happiness, which may include an element of surprise as they are trying to both entertain the audience and entice them to tap their toes and dance along with them.

BLUES. The blues is sultry and sensual. Deep knee bends, full extensions, and long flowing edges characterize this dance. The partners should show their connection by looking at each other, but they may also wish to express longing by looking away from each other and down at times. The dance may have a variety of interpretations, from soulful to longing to sensual.

CHA-CHA. At the international level, the cha-cha is a light dance, with an often flirtatious challenge between the couple. Both skaters should feel as if they are trying to outdo each other. The dance is characterized by its cha-cha rhythm, combined with gentle knee bend and deep lobes.

You can portray and skate each dance in a variety of ways, but if you start with just a few concepts you will build a repertoire of ideas. Use your face, arms, legs, toes, fingers, and general body expression to set your mood.

Dancing is most often thought of as a conversation between two people. Dance teams know that they can work off their partners to express themselves. Therefore, use your partner by looking at him or her. One look can communicate a full range of emotions. The conversation may also be between the skaters and the audience. You may work on these skills without a partner by using your facial movements, arms, and body to portray the dance. Dancers should set the mood as they step onto the ice and take their opening position, and as the music begins to create an overall atmosphere. For a quickstep you may skate confidently onto the ice, whereas for a tango you should take the ice in a totally different manner. As you take your place, your opening position should continue to set the tone. Before a Paso Doble, you may stomp your feet together and skate with sharp arm and leg movements as the music begins. Or before a blues, you may start by looking down and slowly lifting your eyes to look at the audience. Each dance should look completely different from any other from the moment you take the ice until the moment you leave.

While it is almost impossible to go over the top when you are first starting to express on the ice, once you become used to the work, don't confuse big arm moves for expression. When we present in skating rinks, we are aware that we have to make our movements large for all to see. However, some dances are subtle. Your movements need to be crisp and clear so that their deeper subtleties stand out. True expression should come from your heart. Yes, there will be some days when you need to be a better actor than on others, but don't lose sight of the real feelings, so the emotions you portray on the ice will have more depth.

Above all, enjoy your work. Ice dance is the most expressive discipline in the sport. It involves strong basic skills, athleticism, and drama. Work to create strong lines within your body so that your dances will have definition, meaning, and style. You can ice dance for life!

17

Pairs Skating

Over the years I have skated with many partners, both as a junior competitor and in shows. Once, when I skated with Paul Wylie, we had to do pairs spirals. If you have ever done pairs spirals, you know that the woman's leg is aligned below the man's. Paul and I are pretty similar in height. As we did the spiral, I would lift my leg, pushing Paul's up as he struggled to stay balanced. We laugh about it now, but the experience did teach me that you don't want to push up your partner's foot too high because if he falls he is falling on you, and he will not be able to save you.

In earlier chapters, we discussed the elements that were needed to become a strong singles skater. Pairs skating combines all of the elements of singles skating with another person to create overhead lifts, spins, and jumps unique to the discipline. In addition, pairs skaters, like dance or synchronized skaters, must coordinate and unify their movement with a partner. However, unlike the other disciplines, pairs skating has a greater element of danger that thrills the spectator. Although pairs skating is definitely not for the faint of heart, it can be exhilarating to watch and a joy to participate in.

Two consultants helped write this chapter to provide the most accurate information: Sheryl Franks, the 1980 U.S. champion and Olympic team member, and Bobby Martin, former principal with Holiday on Ice. In this chapter, we expand your knowledge of traditional pairs elements such as death spins, pairs spins, and throws. A discussion of lifts for dance and pairs will follow in chapter 18. Each element has its own techniques, but a few general concepts will improve your team and make the elements easier.

Pairs Concepts

All pairs skaters know several necessary elements to succeed in the discipline. These involve being a strong singles skater, knowing how to unify and match your movements, setting a timing and rhythm to your movements, and spending time together off the ice to work on your movements.

Singles Skills

To be a great pairs skater you must also be a strong singles skater. Many skaters go into pairs because they think that they are not great singles skaters. However, the skills you need to be a good pairs skater, such as jumps and spins, must be developed on your own. To make your pairs sit spins low and have strong side-by-side jumps and footwork, you need to know how to execute these skills yourself. To be a truly great pairs team, both skaters must know their roles and work to unify their movements. A good all-around pairs team knows that their pairs elements, such as overhead lifts, must be strong and grand, but that what will really set them apart are the details, like strong singles skating and unison.

Unison

Pairs teams traditionally have a great deal of height difference between the two partners. Some coaches believe this is necessary to achieve the proper height on lifts. However, not all pairs teams have this inequality. Both partners should understand that the man provides the base and the woman helps any throws, assisted jumps, or lifts by maintaining a strong, locked framework. Thus, the woman needs to have very strong positions of her own. Many people believe that only the woman needs to be flexible, but the man also needs to be flexible so that both have greater range of motion in their movements. Both partners need to be able to match each other in terms of leg turnout and height of arm and leg movements.

As most pairs teams have a great height discrepancy, the team needs to work extra-hard on unison. The two types of unison are *exact* and *mirror.* In exact unison, the partners try to match arms, legs, and bodies in position, strength, turnout, and height of movements (figure 17.1). In mirror unison, the couples try to do the mirror opposite of the other, still in terms of body position, strength, turnout, and height of movements. In both types of unison, the partners must be able to follow each other's lead.

I've always been a good copycat. I've found that the biggest help in matching someone is looking at the person. When I first skated pairs I was still pretty young, and I remember it was so hard to look at my partner Bobby in any kind of romantic way. I would just laugh or stop and turn the other

In positions such as this pair spin, both partners must have good positions and match each other in extension and turnout.

way. However, in using your eyes to communicate and express, you are also able to watch and match your partner. It also gives you the connectedness you need to execute intricate spins, lifts, and other maneuvers, so it is extremely important for your unison.

Although you may try to make your routines the same every day and work to repeat the choreography, each day you may feel a little different. If one day your partner takes a deeper edge on a specific move, you should be able to follow. Usually, if one partner's hips are more open than the other partner's, the stronger should try to match the weaker partner in turnout. However, the weaker partner should continue to work on turnout to be as strong as the stronger partner.

Timing

Establishing timing for all elements is vital for successful pairs skating. According to Sheryl Franks, "In a pair that looks new, the mistakes are

Figure 17.1   Exact unison going into a jump.

timing." The team needs to establish a rhythm by bending before the lift or by counting: for example, "one, two, lift" or "one, two, throw." Some skaters also use vocal cues to match their side-by-side spins, and you will hear them say "out" at the end of the spin. This is a good method for learning to unify your movements together. However, it should not be so loud that it is distracting. Timing can be taught, but each pair's version will most likely be slightly different, as all skaters' internal rhythms are unique. That is why combining and unifying elements together is so difficult.

Off-Ice Training

To establish the inner strength and flexibility needed in pairs, the team needs to do a majority of their work off the ice. Most teams spend at least 30 minutes every day that they skate working off-ice on lifts and throws. Working on pairs elements on the floor gives skaters stability and allows them to better work on timing, efficiency of movement, and the specific techniques needed in elements. In addition, both skaters need to be very strong and very flexible. We will talk specifically about off-ice training in part 5, but pairs skaters have a greater element of danger to their work and therefore especially need to perfect their skills. In working on the floor, you should preferably have a space with mats. In addition, you should do things in front of a mirror, as you will see any corrections that need to be made in technique and the look of your movements.

Finally, although we will get into some of the performance aspects in part 6, it is worth noting that pairs skaters need to be definite in their positions. You cannot hide from the audience when you are in an overhead lift. Thus you need to be extremely conscious of the details and articulate your arm, hand, leg, feet, and head positions.

Technique

Although we cannot adequately cover every element needed in pairs skating, we will cover pairs spins, solo spins, death spirals, and jumps here. These are a few of the major elements that every pairs team works to perfect. We will not cover lifts in this chapter, but you will find more specific information on lifts in chapter 18.

Spins

The two types of spins that pairs skaters need to work on are *solo spins* and *pairs spins*. In solo spins, skaters execute the same spin by themselves in a side-by-side alignment. They can do any type of spin they want as long as the spin is synchronized and unified in position. To synchronize their movements, pairs teams need to step into their spins and begin them at exactly the same time. Thus, their setup edge for the spin needs to be precisely unified.

In a pairs spin, both partners need to continue to watch each other as they spin. In the spin, you actually spot your partner. For example, in a flying camel, every time I am facing my partner, I should see his blade. If I don't, I should pull my leg to the side to slow it down or pull it back a little to speed it up so that I'm matching him. The trick is that you need to decide together who will adjust the spin. That way you both are not trying to adjust and making the mismatch worse.

In a pairs spin, the partners usually skate a back crossover and step into the circle toward each other to execute the spin facing each other (figure 17.2). The spin may be in any variation of an upright, camel, or sit spin. In championship-level modern pairs the woman has a great deal of flexibility to create interesting spin variations. The important thing to remember is that any changes of position should not disturb the flow. According to the USFSA Rulebook, both partners must make changes of feet together or separately with uninterrupted flow during the spin. (See the USFSA Rulebook for a complete look at rules and requirements for each level of pairs competition.) Many skaters lose flow on their pairs spin. This could be slightly alleviated if both skaters remember to bend into their push on any changes of position.

Many skaters now do a move where they pull apart and come back together in the middle of the spin. The move can look awkward if it interrupts the flow. It is important for each person to find the elastic feeling within so that when they pull apart they are able to pull back into a fast spin. Each skater needs to keep their muscles taut and pull back into their partner to keep the spin fast (figure 17.3).

Figure 17.2 Stepping into a pairs spin.

Figure 17.3 Pulling apart during the spin as a variation.

It is also important that the spin entrance be well timed together so that the skaters don't bump into each other on the entrance. In the spin, the positions should be clean and well defined. If it is a pairs sit, the woman should have a straight back. Or in a camel pairs spin, each skater should have strong positions with their arms, legs, and heads.

Death Spirals

Ludmila and Oleg Protopopov, the 1964 and 1968 Olympic gold medalists, first made death spirals famous. In the death spiral, the man pivots in one plane while the woman moves in a wide arc around him into a position low to the ice. Death spirals may be done with the woman facing forward or backward on outside or inside edges. To set up the death spiral, the skaters generally start face to face with the man holding the woman's hand. He holds her hand with his skating hand and bends both knees with his back leg centering into a pivot.

Death spirals are difficult to learn in the beginning, but they are easier if you and your partner trust each other and use each other to pull against. If you don't have the pull and elastic stretch between you, the woman will fall on the ice as she tries to go down. There must be a connected pull between you and your partner so that the woman can use the centrifugal force to get into the death spiral.

You can use a couple of different grips as you go into it. I like to have my palm on the inside so that I have something to press against and use my strength to lean on him (figure 17.4). It almost feels as if we are holding wrists. If we don't have a good hold, we will not have enough tension for the move.

The woman must be on a solid edge. Death spirals are named for her edge, not the man's, so on a backward outside death spiral she is on a back outside edge. The woman is not allowed to touch the ice with any part of

Figure 17.4 This is one of several possible death spiral grips.

Figure 17.5   Keeping the body aligned in one piece in the entrance to the death spiral.

her body as a way to steady herself. Therefore, it is very important that she keep her body in one aligned piece as she approaches the finished position (figure 17.5). She needs to make sure that her hips are pressed up and away from the ice toward the ceiling so that her back will have a nice arch. She also needs to keep her hips square with her body so that the force of the edge does not disturb her base, causing her to roll off the edge.

On the back outside, skaters often bend to get into the position. Your knee should not be locked as you go in, but there is really no reason to bend both knees as you go down. If you hold your shoulder back and really press up so that you have a curved body, you can use the pressure and tension of your hold and the edge to go right into the death spiral. In addition, you should remember to keep your knees closed to keep the free hip lifted.

Many variations may be done in death spirals in terms of the position of both skaters' free arms and the woman's free leg and head. Generally, both skaters should work to create clear, definite lines in their bodies in this position. Death spirals can be truly beautiful when they are executed cleanly and clearly (figure 17.6).

Jumps and Throws

Pairs skaters do two types of jumps: *side-by-side jumps* and *throws*. Side-by-side jumps are exactly how they sound: Each skater executes a solo jump, but the pair must unify their takeoffs so that they land at the same time. The jumps should be performed close together so that they look unified. An additional element may enter in if the skaters jump in different directions.

Figure 17.6 Full death spiral position.

In this instance, the takeoff and landing still need to be unified even though each skater is jumping in the opposite direction.

Throw jumps sound scary, but they are really partner-assisted jumps in which the man takes the woman's free hand and skating hip to propel her into any regular jump. They really shouldn't be called throw jumps because the man doesn't literally hurl the woman. His role is to assist the woman so that she can get greater spring and height in the air. Most often these include Axels, Salchows, and loops. The woman must land solidly over her skating side on one foot. The extra force of the jump often makes this difficult to land, but the man is only allowed to assist in the takeoff, not the landing (figure 17.7a).

In the air, the woman must pull into her usual rotational position with hands to chest and ankles neatly crossed (figure 17.7b). As she lands, she needs to make sure that she is on a bent knee and that she checks her free side forward to stop the rotation (figure 17.7c). In addition, if her free hip is too high on the landing, she will slip off her edge. So she needs to level her hips as she lands. On the landing, many skaters lift the free leg immediately. It is better, as we discussed previously, to land the jump first with a solid check and then lift the leg. That way you will not teeter forward on your blade and fall on the landing.

Pairs skating can be an exciting and challenging discipline. As you work on the elements, try to add your own variation and style to make them your own. It is your distinctive rhythm and timing that will set you apart from the rest, providing you and your partner the opportunity to show off your individual talents and your skills as a team.

Figure 17.7 Throw jump: *(a)* assisted takeoff, *(b)* moving to the in-air position, and *(c)* landing.

18

Basic Lifts

In the past two chapters we talked about pairs and ice dance. Although these two disciplines have their own unique attributes, they share a common element: lifts. Most often we think of pairs lifts as being overhead and dance lifts as being beneath the man's shoulders, but pairs skaters borrow lifts and ideas from dancers and vice versa. All lifts require that the man be on balance and that he have efficient foot placement, and that the woman not only make the lift look effortless but also assist the man. Whether you are the lifter or the one being lifted, in this chapter we will improve your knowledge of your role and give you a few lift examples from each discipline. Remember, lifts should be successfully executed several times off the ice with a coach's supervision before they are ever tried with skates on.

Lift Concepts

Lifts can be fun, but they can also be a bit scary if you don't know what you are doing. When we are young, we are less afraid of being lifted and possibly dropped. However, eventually most women realize how high they are off the ice, and many men realize that they could trip and drop the woman, and fear sets in. Before you begin any lift, it is important that both partners know what they will be doing. Recently, I was asked to do a lift in a show with some of the best male pairs and dancers. I was told that two guys would be lifting me and one would be there to catch me. Without much instruction, they picked me up by my ankle and calf and lifted me until I was standing above them. For a second, I was so scared and I wasn't sure what to do. I fell back. Luckily, Vladimir Besedin was there to catch me. He was surprised that I knew that he would be there. However, I had a lot of trust in all of them, and knew that they wouldn't lift me without having a plan, even if I didn't know what it was. In this situation, everything worked out. Keep in mind, however, that it's OK to ask questions. Know what you will be doing and make sure that you are both very clear about your roles.

Beautiful lift positions thrill the audience and showcase the couple's skills.

Individual Roles

You may occasionally skate with someone who is very experienced in lifting others. After the 1994 Olympics, I was really good friends with Olympic pairs champion Artur Dmitriev. He was teaching me Russian and I was teaching him English. He taught me several lifts off ice that I'd never done before. Artur is so strong that he could move me into a position in the air. However, no matter how he lifted me, I knew that I needed to keep my body tight and strong. Lifts are very deceptive because they always look as if the man is doing all the work. Actually, lifts are an equal relationship, with both partners starting the lift, maintaining its position in the air, and executing a smooth setdown. If the woman does her part and holds the position properly, she is able to take about ten pounds off her body weight.

When you are learning a lift, it is best to get into a position and stay there, even if it's wrong—you can always fix it later. Pairs skaters must always fight to hold their bodies tight to stay in a compact position. If the woman is too loose, the man can feel as if he is lifting heavy, wet noodles, and it will be harder for him to control the lift. So it is very important for the woman to keep whatever position she is in as she is being lifted. Doing so will help the man tremendously.

The woman needs to have a very strong position in the air, and the man needs to have solid footwork. The man is the base of movement in any lift. As such, he needs to be very stable and solid on his feet. He must know where his feet will be placed and how he will place them, articulating his toe point and flex to create very smooth turns. In addition, when adding 85 to 125 pounds above him, it is a lot harder to catch his balance if he is off. This is important not only for him but also for the confidence of the woman. If she hears toe picks scratching below and feels that her partner does not solidly have her, she will not want to practice lifts. To that end, the man should do isolated continuous mohawks or threes down the length of the ice (figure 18.1). He should be on the ball of the foot, but not so far forward that he would hit his toes. To increase the rotational speed, he needs

Figure 18.1 Men should practice doing mohawks down the ice to solidify the strength of their foot movements.

to keep his feet tight and close together. For a slower pace, he needs to widen his stance. If he is able to do them impeccably well on his own, he will be able to do them with a partner.

The man's knees become very important in lifting. According to Collin Sullivan, many men are told to "bend to pick up the woman." As a result, the man bends from the waist to pick up his partner, stressing and straining the lower back. Instead, the man should lower his knees, keeping his spine straight to pick up the woman and put her down (figure 18.2). He should also remember to lift her on the way up. It sounds silly, but many men don't lift the woman until she is coming down, again putting undue stress and strain on the body. The woman should be lifted close to the man's body. He should not have to reach away from his body to hold her. Just as you would carry suitcases close to your body for ease, the lifts should pass as close to the man's center as possible. As he lifts the woman, the man will feel his abdominal muscles activate. This keeps his body in one consistent plane, providing balance and support for the lift.

On the setdown, the man needs to bend his knees, not his waist. In lowering from the knees, he will help her to find the ice. The woman needs to find the ball of her foot so that she does not clunk down on her blade or

Figure 18.2 As the man lifts the woman into a dance lift, he must bend his knees and keep his back straight, lifting through the legs.

Figure 18.3 At the set down of the lift, the woman bends into her skating knee to maintain the couple's flow.

go over her toe pick. She also needs to bend into her skating knee so that she will maintain the couple's flow (figure 18.3). In addition, she should use her back and abdominal muscles to put her body back into its proper alignment.

Generally, both partners also need to think about how the lift looks. Although the man is the base, his movements will not go unnoticed. The woman is usually the highlight of the lift, so she needs to make sure that she has a well-stretched and clear position, but both partners should have stretched backs and necks. Especially in pairs overhead lifts, the woman is high above the ice. She should look strong, with a nice, long neck, her shoulders pressed down, her position stretched, her abdominal muscles and glutes tight. Both members of the team need to work together to make a lift that feels and appears easy, fluid, and attractive.

Preparation and Training

As you try anything new, you should be extremely cautious. Don't feel that you are taking the easy way out. It is important to do any lifts off the ice before taking them onto the ice. Many training centers require that their pairs do at least 30 minutes of off-ice lifting a day. Both skaters are somewhat in jeopardy in a lift and need to be aware that until they fully understand the motion and timing, they are putting themselves in danger. When you try lifts on the ice, you are adding many variables: balance, the condition of the ice, the weight of your and your partner's skates, and general confusion. So perfect your lifts off the ice on mats in front of mirrors, if possible, before taking them onto the ice. Mirrors allow you to see how the lifts look and will show whether either partner is blocking the other within the execution. Some rinks do not have mirrors that are high enough for pairs skaters to see themselves in the lift. The Plexiglas can be very helpful as you often can see your reflection in the glass when on the ice. Here again it is helpful to have a man coach to show the man how to do his part and a woman coach to show the woman how to do her part. Practicing the lift with someone who has done it many times before will give you greater knowledge and confidence when you try it with your regular partner.

Once you learn the lift, it is important to maintain a daily off-ice schedule, as you will constantly be working to perfect it. Also, your internal rhythm is a little different every day, so you need to retrain and reteach your body every day. You will have a certain amount of muscle memory, but it is better to check this muscle memory off the ice rather than on it.

Dance Lifts

Figure 18.4 In-air position of the assisted waltz jump.

Competitive ice dancers have two modes of lifting: *assisted jumps* and *dance lifts*. The man is not allowed to raise his hands above his shoulders in either lift, so ice dancers can only do overhead lifts in show programs.

An example of an assisted jump is a waltz jump done in closed (waltz) hold. In this jump, the woman steps from the back outside edge to the forward outside and does a waltz jump with the man's assistance. Her right hand and his left are in a traditional waltz hold. The only difference is that his left hand and her right lowers to her hip level so that he can push her up and into the air once she has jumped (figure 18.4). She lands on a back outside edge and the move can be repeated if she steps forward and jumps again.

Lifts may be done either in traditional holds or nontraditional holds. An example of a traditional lift would begin with both partners skating side by side in open or foxtrot position. The woman should wrap her left arm around the man's back so that her left armpit is over the man's right shoulder. Both partners bend into their knees and the woman springs into the air as they stand up. In the air, the woman has a variety of options, such as bending both knees back into a double attitude (as in figure 18.5) or straightening both legs with one forward so that she looks as if she is in the splits from the side.

An example of a nontraditional hold involves both the man and woman skating either forward or

Figure 18.5 In-air position of a traditional hold.

backward with her back facing his chest. She bends one knee into attitude so that her foot wraps around the man's back. She keeps her free leg lifted and turned out. The man reaches around her waist with his skating arm. With his free arm, he has two options: to grab over or to grab under the woman's free leg. If he grabs over, the woman will lean, changing the shape of the lift. The woman may vary her skating leg in a number of ways. She could join it with her free knee in a double attitude, wrap it around the other side of the man's back, point it straight down toward the ice, or lift it straight up in the air so that she's in the splits with either both legs bent or one leg held in attitude and the free leg straight (figure 18.6). In the lift, the couple should bend together, and he should set her down in the same position that he lifted her in on either direction on either edge.

Figure 18.6 In-air position of a nontraditional hold.

Pairs Lifts

Pairs lifts are generally broken down into three handhold positions: *hand-to-hand*, *hand-to-waist*, and *hand-to-armpit*. In each of these handholds, countless variations are possible as changing the entrance or exit can greatly alter the lift.

An example of a hand-to-hand hold is the press lift (figure 18.7). In the press lift, the man skates backward with the woman forward. The woman's arms are fairly straight, with her hands at about hip level. The man's hands are underneath her and he presses her up over his head. She finishes with both legs in a V shape overhead. The lift may also be executed as a dance lift, with the woman low so that her feet are only about a foot off the ice. As the woman assists into this lift, she needs to think of going up and over the man, almost in a curve instead of just straight up. That will help her put her center of gravity over his. In addition, the man shouldn't look at her as she goes up. Doing so may disturb his balance and he could go back on his heels. In the lift, both partners need to make sure that they keep their shoulders down using their back muscles. If they do not, the lift has a droopy look in the air. The man also needs to remember to keep his arms up near his ears, not too far forward or back, with his elbows bent. In addition, the man has to be sure not to squeeze his partner's hands. He should use the heel of his palm, rather than his fingers, to maintain contact.

A variation on the hand-to-hand lift is the lasso. In a lasso, the partners begin by skating face to face. The man is holding the woman's hands and she jumps as if doing a waltz jump. She may also do this jump with a toe assist. He then swings her from his front to behind as he rotates and sets her down on a back edge. As this lift involves complicated positioning, both partners must keep their bodies in alignment. They also need to make sure that they are together in their timing and rhythm.

Figure 18.7 In-air position of the press lift.

An example of the hand-to-waist hold is the star lift (figure 18.8). The man and woman face each other on the takeoff and the man holds the woman's hand in his. She puts one hand on his shoulder. He puts his hand on her waist and they bend and spring into the air. In the air, the woman's other arm is stretched. The woman can either stretch both legs or stretch one leg and bend the other. In either case, she should point her toes and make the leg positions clear. In this lift it is important that both partners are comfortable with his hand placement on her waist. If it is too high, he will squeeze her ribs, which is very uncomfortable for the woman. It is hard to make the position the same every time, but the woman should feel very stable in the hold. If the hold is right, she should just be resting. He should feel that he is holding her, but not squeezing in any way.

Figure 18.8 In-air position of the star lift.

Another type of hand-to-waist lift is the twist lift. To start the twist lift, both skaters are backward. The man holds the woman by the waist (figure 18.9a). She puts her hands on his wrists. She toes in and, as she springs from the ice, he assists her into the air (figure 18.9b). In the air, she will rotate between one half to three and a half times. The man rotates forward to catch her by the waist and set her down on the ice. This lift has many variations, as the woman may also briefly delay the jump with a split before she tightens into her rotation. The twist may either be a straight vertical twist or it may be slightly tipped so that the woman is almost parallel to the ice, making it a lateral twist lift. This is a very advanced move and should only be practiced after learning the proper technique with a coach. As you work on it, remember to keep your elbows in. Any changes in your position or timing can have dangerous effects. Once I did the split twist with my partner and

a   b

Figure 18.9   The twist lift *(a)* pick-up position, and *(b)* in the air before the twist.

the jump was bigger than we usually did it, so I finished rotating too early. I landed in front of his face and broke his nose. There is a process to learning the timing, so it should be perfected off the ice first, and always with the woman's feet and elbows in tight to her body!

An example of the hand-to-armpit hold is the Axel lift. In this lift, the man starts backward with the woman on a forward outside edge. The man grabs her under her armpits. As she springs, he straightens his elbows so that his arms are fully extended. He rotates and sets her down on a back outside edge on one foot. This lift can be particularly beautiful in the air if the woman continues to press her shoulders down. Many women allow their back muscles to release, so their shoulders pop up around their ears and the stretch in their necks and backs is not visible.

As you work to perfect your lifts, above all else, work with sense, supervision, and caution. If each partner tries to maintain strong positions, working on timing and technique, your lifts will create interesting positions with a sense of ease and control.

19

Synchronized Skating

Although skaters have long skated in groups for shows or their own enjoyment, the sport of synchronized skating did not start drawing attention until the 1980s. Skaters who felt that they didn't have a strong competitive future in the other disciplines turned to synchro, then called *precision*. The sport, considered less athletic and more like show skating than competitive skating, was not readily recognized by the other disciplines.

In the last twenty years, synchro has encouraged numerous skaters who otherwise might have quit to stay with skating. Legions of athletic, artistic, and dedicated teams have entirely changed the sport's image. It is considered the fastest-growing discipline in skating today. Top nationally known freestylists and ice dancers compete with teams in events like the World Synchronized Skating Championships. The sport combines the other disciplines, employing techniques that are used in freestyle, pairs, dance, and Moves in the Field. Although skating fans are still learning the merits of synchro, the skaters who partake in this exciting discipline have long enjoyed the camaraderie of working in a team.

Like any team sport athletes, synchronized skaters know that they are only as strong as their weakest member. In this chapter, we will give you the skills that you need to become a successful synchronized skater, looking specifically at individual skating skills and presentation. To provide the most accurate information, Lynn Benson, a pioneer in the sport of synchro and coach of two of the sport's top teams, the Haydenettes (11-time national senior champions) and the Ice Mates (11-time national novice champions and two-time intermediate champions), has contributed to this chapter. As we will explain, although you may think that you can work on your team skills only with your team, you can always improve your individual skating and therefore become a better team skater.

Being a Strong Link

A team cannot succeed if every member is not a strong individual skater. Whenever a skater comes to rely on the rest of the team to supply power, edges, or presentation, she has let the group down. To that end, each skater must be able to skate the routine competently on her own. She must have strong stroking, deep edges, control, speed, and intricate footwork. In addition, she should be able to skate with good posture and individual alignment so that when she takes hold with her team members, she will not use the various holds to steady herself.

Just as a team's program must present a well-balanced technical impression overall, each skater must have a strong skating background in the areas of dance, Moves in the Field, and freestyle. As the technical bar has been raised, the quality of each individual skater's skills has also had to improve. Some teams now require that their members pass certain test levels in dance, freestyle, and Moves in the Field. Lynn Benson requires these tests for team members and also expects freestyle proficiency, as single jumps and spins

© Sue Rosario

Each skater on a synchronized team must develop strong individual skills, such as these spirals.

are permissible in competition. Benson looks for solid basic skills during tryouts and says that she spends the longest time looking at skaters' individual skills. She asks skaters to do Ina Bauers, lunges, spirals, spread eagles, jumps, spins, some acceleration drills, and a step sequence consisting of choctaws, brackets, rockers, or other basic footwork. She says that she purposely keeps tryouts rather simplistic, as the harder things can be learned if a skater has a strong skating foundation. She primarily looks for speed, deep edges, style, and flexibility.

Elements and Transitions

As a team, synchronized members are required to execute circles, lines, blocks, wheels, and intersections. Junior- and Senior-level teams compete in both a long and a short program. Each maneuver must be executed cleanly and in unison. Therefore, synchronized skaters must have precise footwork, as one sloppy foot placement could result in a chain reaction fall, disrupting the team. The skaters must work to unify their movements. Unlike dancers or pairs skaters, who work to match one partner, synchronized skaters must work to match up to 20 others depending on their level. (For specific rules on age requirements, number of skaters allowed, and rules, see the USFSA

Used by permission of Lynn Benson

Circles, and variations on them, are a required element in synchronized competition.

Rulebook.) To that end, the team must unify their head, arm, body, and leg movements in length, height, and turnout. For example, a smaller skater might have a different natural extension than a taller skater, so they must work to match their movements.

While teams must cleanly execute the major elements, they also need interesting connecting moves between them. Just as freestyle programs of all crossovers between jumps are boring to watch, a team that can do wonderful maneuvers but has little happening between them will not do well competitively. The transitions have become just as important as the elements themselves. Creativity, deep knee bend, speed, and edges are needed for smooth transitions. As in dance, skaters must use their legs and hips to create edges and turns. In doing so, they use their backs to control their movements so that they will not disrupt their upper bodies and holds.

To raise the level of skating and add to the excitement, jumps, spins, and certain types of lifts are now permissible in synchro. The jumps consist of half-revolution jumps, such as waltzes and falling leaves in the short program, and singles such as flips or loops in the long program. Mostly upright spins such as scratch spins and laybacks have been done thus far, but sit spins and camel spins have also made rare appearances. According to Benson, flying sits or butterflies could be in the sport's future. Thus, skaters must work on their spins and jumps so that they can be done quickly within elements or transitions and do not require a long setup time. As most skaters jump left to right, skaters who usually jump right to left may have to relearn their jumps and spins so that they will be synchronized with their team-mates. The days of teams executing maneuvers on two feet are over. Strong skaters must have coordination and speed to do all maneuvers in a variety of holds and footwork positions.

Presentation

While elements and transitions make up the base of the program, the presentation of those elements gives each team its individuality. The elements need to cover the full ice surface and reflect the music in a distinctive and original way.

Once the music is chosen and the choreography is set, the skaters must know their individual parts inside and out. To check this, Benson has the team do the entire routine together without holding on to ensure that no one is relying on teammates. If the skaters do not have sufficient upper-body strength, they start gripping or leaning on their teammates. Although this problem is sometimes difficult to see, the team will have an overall sloppy or disconnected appearance. To build upper-body strength, Benson says that she has the members skate through the program detached, and "Any time they're in the shoulder grip I make them keep their arms a little higher than their shoulders." In this instance, the skaters must use their lats and

Synchronized skaters need upper body strength to help them hold up their arms and not lean on each other.

back muscles to hold their arms instead of the smaller muscles in their arms and shoulders. If each skater can skate with the arms higher than the shoulders, keeping the shoulders pressed down, they all will use their upper body in shoulder holds, and will be less fatigued by the end of the routine and less likely to lean on teammates.

Another important aspect of presentation is expression. Each skater needs to use the body and face to set a mood during the routine. While skating is a sport, it's also an art form. The best synchronized teams recognize this and use arms, legs, bodies, and faces to augment routines. We will cover this more in chapter 24. The difference in skating with a team is that not every member portrays expression the same way, and some skaters may never feel comfortable expressing. Coach Benson advises that skaters work on this together in front of mirrors. Each part of the program should have a specific style and expression that the team as a whole is trying to achieve. Thus, each skater should work individually on this as well.

Teams also need to be unified with the music. To be truly one with the music, skaters need to feel it, paying attention to musical nuances and details. Synchronized skaters, like skaters in the other disciplines, should have a copy of their music that they listen to on a daily basis. Skaters should listen to their music, visualizing in three ways: as a skater doing the routine, as a spectator watching the team, and as a judge marking the team.

Facial expression is an important factor in a team's presentation.

Visualizing reinforces positive execution of the routine in your mind and is a tool that is used by many different kinds of athletes and performers. As a synchronized skater, you need to know that you can execute the routine's elements to the best of your ability individually and with your team members.

Benson reinforces this idea with her team. She does not push them for medals, but instead strives for consistency in skating. "We have never swayed from our goal, which is to put together an entertaining program that is strong, technically difficult, and creative, and skate it cleanly." To that end, she asks her skaters to think of one element at a time, not moving on to the next element in their minds until they have finished the current maneuver. She also reminds them that, while they are being judged, they skate for the audience and want the audience to be pleased and amazed by what they see.

Synchronized Athletes

To achieve the proper techniques and presentation that are required on the ice, synchronized skaters need to develop an off-ice training program. We will cover off-ice training in greater detail in part 5, but skaters must know that they are athletes. Like all skaters, synchronized teams should work on off-ice strength, conditioning, and flexibility to gain balance, coordination, strength, and overall body fitness. To that end, skaters on the Haydenettes work with a trainer to develop their own individual strength and conditioning programs. The team also has a warm-up routine that they do together before they skate practices and a specialized routine for competitions. On ice, they spend the first 15 minutes with a warm-up and have a mandatory power and edge class every week.

Like any athlete, skaters need to be aware that what they do off the ice affects their on-ice ability. If they arrive at practices tired and hungry, they are letting themselves and their teammates down and will probably be less effective in that day's practice. Synchronized skating is no longer a small part of figure skating. It is a year-round endeavor, requiring awareness and commitment by the coaches and skaters. According to Benson, "Just as in any discipline, synchro coaches have to stay current with the latest trends and rules. So in the offseason, you should attend synchro camps, seminars, and conferences."

As the sport of synchro grows, there is no doubt that the technical abilities and requirements will rise. As long as you work on your individual skills and pay attention to the trends, you will remain a quality skater who is in synch with the fastest-growing discipline in the sport.

Part 5

Training
Off the Ice

Over the years, I have found that work off the ice has been crucial to my development as a skater and overall conditioning as an athlete. After I was injured in 1994, I sought out the help of well-known trainer Dr. Igor Burdenko, who received his doctorate in human performance in the former Soviet Union. Dr. Burdenko has worked not only with skaters like Paul Wylie and me but also with many different professional and recreational athletes, dancers, and people who are working to overcome traumatic injuries. His clients have participated in every Olympics since 1984. Through his unique training methods combining land and water exercises, he has even helped people who once were considered paralyzed to walk, prompting some to give him the nickname "the Miracle Man."

When I first met Dr. Burdenko, I could barely walk. I had about five weeks to prepare for the Olympics, the biggest athletic event a skater could imagine, yet I couldn't skate. Our work began very gently but aggressively, with non–weight-bearing exercises in the pool. My knee quickly improved, and once I found that I could move more freely, we started doing very difficult exercises. We used the water as a gym not only to swim but also to stretch and perform different exercises and even my programs with the music. Dr. Burdenko believes in six essential qualities for success in any exercise program: balance, coordination, flexibility, endurance, speed/quickness, and strength. We worked on all of these skills not only in the water but also on the land. Despite all that was happening at that time, Dr. Burdenko's interesting exercises and infectious positive personality actually made it fun to work out. In the process, I had fun, and my whole body was in the best shape ever. As a result, the experience in 1994 became much more positive than I could have possibly imagined.

Even now, I return to these exercises to keep myself in shape. Once, when I went back on tour after a break, several people commented to me that I was in great shape. My music was 3 minutes and 46 seconds long, and I kept skating the whole routine in every practice. After a few days of everyone telling me how great I looked and commenting on my improved endurance, I finally had to confess that I'd really only skated about three times in four weeks. Everyone was shocked because they all had been skating about four times a day. I later explained to them that I had been exercising daily to keep my muscles in tone, but between spending time with my family and other commitments, I hadn't had time to skate. Of course, I don't recommend that you stop skating. However, this proves that if you know what exercises you need to work on to keep yourself strong and in shape, your off-ice work will benefit your skating. Some skaters and coaches believe that off-ice programs should compose 60 percent of your training program, with only 40 percent of your time on the ice. Although this may seem a bit drastic, I find that in working all my muscles, not just the ones needed for skating, my balance and coordination on the ice stays the same as if I had been skating daily.

In this section you will learn how to build an off-ice training program that works for you individually. We will cover general off-ice principles, warming up and cooling down, cross-training ideas, and a few exercises. Dr. Burdenko served as a consultant for this section, as did noted exercise physiologist and certified personal trainer Jessica Regnante.

As you begin reading the chapters in this section, keep in mind that each skater's body is different. Two skaters who are the same age, level, and height may have entirely different muscle development. We have tried to take this into account, offering tips to make each skill harder or easier. As you work, you must be careful. Err on the side of caution when possible. Because even elite athletes can have undiagnosed health problems, you should consult your physician any time you begin a new exercise program. You should also have your coach or a trainer work with you as you do these exercises to make sure you are doing them correctly. Do them in front of mirrors to check your posture and alignment. Above all, pay attention to your body. These exercises may make you work different muscles than you are used to. If you have any pain, stop immediately and have a qualified professional check that you are doing them correctly. Remember that the idea is to augment your on-ice program, not cause additional problems. Therefore, work hard, but work smart. These skills will transfer to the ice if done correctly and will make you a better skater.

20

Off-Ice Training Concepts

When I worked with Dr. Burdenko, I learned a new way of training. We worked mostly in the pool in the beginning. When you're working in the pool, you don't realize how hard you are working, but when you're finished, you feel it! According to a survey, 50 exercise physiologists at major universities agreed that walking for 30 minutes in the water is equivalent to walking for two hours on land. Once I began to feel better, we increased our time on the land so that we worked equally in the water and on land. As you will see, the exercises that we worked on were very efficient. They always worked more than one muscle group at a time and they taught me that exercise is a thinking process that requires the same kind of intensity as skating. In this chapter, I will explain some of the major concepts of Dr. Burdenko's method, adding my own insights on the importance of working out and specific things that skaters should keep in mind. If you practice these skills, you will find that your workouts will not only become more intense, but you will also be very efficient in your training and you will become a better skater.

Skaters and Working Out

As skaters, we often think of working out as jogging or doing some sort of cardio work and lifting weights. Most gyms are made up of machines, and the emphasis is on training for endurance and strength. I've found that when I lift weights, it makes me too strong and my muscles become too bulky, losing the quickness that is needed for jumps, spins, and fast timing in choreography. I did discover that the most important thing to work on in training is the abdominal muscles. Strong abdominals, back, and arms are important for the proper timing in jumps.

Once, I landed a triple Lutz practically sideways at a world championships, and Paul Duchesnay, former ice dancing world champion, came up to me and said, "Wow, you could be an ice dancer with edges like that!" I had landed leaning way out on the edge, but because I used my abdominal muscles I was able to stand up and save it. Some skaters use weights sparingly for their legs, performing many repetitions with light weights. I found that through using exercise tubing and resistance, I was better able to work my muscles in the ways I needed for skating. If I worked with weights too often and got too muscular, my timing was slow. In addition, working out with weights can be very dangerous for younger skaters or skaters who have not been properly trained. In working out with resistance, if you find that the work is too hard, you simply move closer so that the resistance decreases.

Six Essential Training Qualities

In lifting weights, you perform a static activity. Skating is definitely not static; it's all about movement. So you want to work on skills off the ice that will help, not hinder, your work on the ice. When I worked with Dr. Burdenko, he taught me that working with equipment and weights is a way of disintegrating the body. Skaters need to do things that integrate the body and teach it to move together. In addition, as he says, "When you work with machines you come to depend on the machine and you perform primarily in a sitting position. It's not a functional position. The human body is designed to be vertical and jump and walk." Through his work with rehabilitation, conditioning, and training, he has focused on six essential qualities that he believes are necessary to any training program and everyday activities. The qualities are balance, coordination, flexibility, endurance, speed/quickness, and strength. If you think of these qualities as a pyramid, you can visualize them as in figure 20.1.

Balance is the foundation of all sports. Figure skaters know that they must have balance to skate. Dr. Burdenko worked on my posture in the water and on land to increase my ability to balance. Next, we worked on *coordination*. As Dr. Burdenko says, "You can't be flexible if you aren't coordinated." He

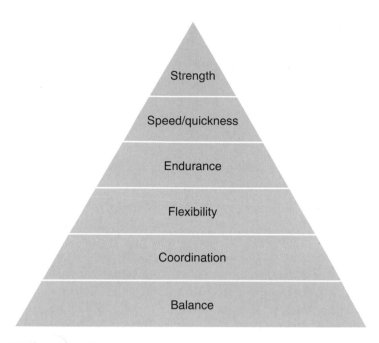

Figure 20.1 Six essential training qualities.

encourages people to smile as they train because he says that when you smile, you relax about 250 muscles. Doing so makes you less stiff and more coordinated. Next, we worked on *flexibility*, then moved into *endurance* and *speed and quickness.* Speed relates to the rate of your motion, and quickness relates to your ability to use your reflexes to prompt action. Finally, we worked on *strength.* The pyramid is very logical. If a weightlifter doesn't have balance, he will not be able to use his strength. No matter how strong you are you must also have a solid base of balance and coordination. If you flip the pyramid upside down, it will not be able to stand up, so balance is crucial to your training—especially since skaters perform on a quarter-inch of steel on ice.

In his book *Overcoming Paralysis,* coauthored with Scott Biehler (1999, Avery Publishing Group), Dr. Burdenko explains that he also follows four other main principles:

1. Work out in the water and on the land.
2. Work in the vertical position. In working vertically, your body is given the signal that it is time to work. Vertical is also a functional position.
3. Work the whole body, not just parts, and work in multiple directions at three speeds: slow, medium, and fast.
4. Work not only indoors but also outdoors. We spend so much time in skating rinks, in gyms, and generally inside, that we don't get enough

fresh air, nor do we use all of the outdoor elements that are available to us to keep the workouts interesting and less repetitive. Fresh air is necessary for better body performance. If our oxygen level drops down, we begin to feel tired. Likewise, if you always do the same kinds of exercises, your workouts will not only be boring, but you may also be at risk for injury caused by overuse and microtears in your muscles.

In working both outdoors and indoors, using all of Dr. Burdenko's principles, you can make your workouts more intense and fun.

Water Workouts

Water has incredible healing powers. The reason is that in the water, with the help of a flotation device your muscles do not have to deal with the forces of gravity. As Dr. Burdenko says, "When you are in the water, especially in the deep end, you stop fighting gravitation. You save a tremendous amount of energy." In the water, our bodies are able to relax. As Dr. Burdenko points out, when people go for a vacation, they often go to places near water to recuperate. In many religions, water is used for baptisms, and our bodies are 90 percent water. Water provides support, assistance, and resistance.

You can also use water as a gym to work on the six essential qualities. Just as we use gyms and equipment to develop different muscles, we can use water to develop our bodies. With Dr. Burdenko I worked with a buoyancy vest so that I would not touch the bottom. A buoyancy vest is a special jacket which provides sufficient flotation and can be adjusted to suit any exercise. When you wear it, your shoulders should be above the water so that the water is not level with your face. When properly worn, the vest allows you to work efficiently, using the water as a way to stretch and for balance, coordination, and flexibility, but also for resistance and strength exercises. With the vest, it didn't matter whether I could swim. I felt comfortable and could simply work.

As skaters, we are often told to stay away from pools before a competition because it is believed that too much time in the water can make you too loose. Actually, the opposite is true. In the water we are able to relax and use the water to decrease muscle tension. Before a competition we often train up to the very last minute, and we face mental and physical stress. Through stretching in the water and exercising, we are able to relieve stress and remove the tension that develops through training, allowing our bodies to work more efficiently. Of course, you do not want to stay in the water for more than an hour. By staying in tune with our bodies, we will know when it is time to come out of the water and when we've had enough. We also don't want to simply sit in the pool, for the same reason that we don't want to lie around on the couch for hours. We use the pool as another place for exercise to increase circulation, to speed up our recovery process, and to relax.

Training Smart

Dr. Burdenko often mentions that training is a process of intelligence. We have to be in tune with our bodies to know how hard to push them. As skaters, we are used to listening to our coaches and putting aside our own feelings. We are taught very early on that we have to be tough when we fall and get up and keep going to work through or ignore pain. There are times in performance that you cannot allow a small fall to disturb your momentum. However, if it is a fall that is more than a stumble or a minor jump fall and we try to keep going, we risk long-term injury. We must use our skills and our awareness to pay attention to our bodies. Our coaches and trainers are not inside our bodies, so they don't know how we really feel. Only we know that. As Dr. Burdenko says, "Pain is a language; it is a way that your body and mind communicate to you." It should not be ignored. We must learn to listen to our bodies and respond properly. Often we turn to medicine for relief from pain. Although pain medications are important sometimes, in general these keep your energy level down, making it harder for you to skate. If you listen to your body and participate in your training, you will notice problems or pain from the beginning to prevent them from becoming worse.

Every time we take the ice or work out, we feel a little different. One day our muscles might be tighter or more relaxed, we may be facing outside stresses, or we may feel happy or sad. Many skaters attempt to do the same exercises every day. However, in doing so, they actually risk injury. In working out, you need to target your weaknesses and work to correct them, but you don't want to work only that area. You need to work all of the muscles around it and the whole body. Pay attention not only to when it is hurt but also when it's not hurt. As Dr. Burdenko says, "It is much easier to prevent than to cure." In addition, try not to hit your physical limits. Training to become a good skater is a long process and requires almost daily work. You do not want to train to your absolute limits every day because you may not be able to work the next day.

In working through a balanced off-ice training program that combines all of the essential qualities, it is a good idea to hire a trainer. A trainer oversees your movements to make sure that you are correctly attempting each skill. Many skaters do not use trainers, feeling that they are too expensive. While this is understandable, remember that in doing something right the first time, you will save money because you won't have to hire someone to fix bad habits.

As you select someone to train you, keep in mind that it is important to work with someone who understands skating. The trainer needs to know what movements you do on ice so that he or she can show you exercises and design a program that will closely relate to skating. You do not have to work with him or her daily. While it is ideal to see your trainer a few times a week, due to time and expense you may be able to see him or her only once a month. Even a once or twice a month hourly session is better than none to develop the proper skills. As each athlete's body is different, a trainer can work specifically on your areas of strength and weakness to improve your overall body condition.

As you work on and off the ice, always work safely and efficiently. The skills that you work on and practice off the ice directly relate to the skills you practice on the ice, so listen to your body and work in a safe, relaxed, and consistent manner. Doing so will make you not only a better skater but also a better athlete overall.

21

Warming Up and Cooling Down

With the loss of figures, some say that we are now seeing more injuries because skaters do not warm up adequately. Although I agree that figures did help to partially prepare skaters for freestyle, even then most skaters did not warm up. We mostly changed our skates and then went to free skate. Maybe we stretched on the boards a little, but the positions weren't necessarily for the muscles that we would use and we didn't hold them long enough. For a stretch to be effective, it should be at least 15 to 30 seconds with proper breathing.

When I was younger, I didn't stretch before or after practice sessions. I really regret that now because it is harder to get into the habit when you get older. However, now I worry about injuries and I have to pay attention to stretching before and after the session. After a session, your muscles are tight and contracted. You've used them, so they've worked hard, and they need to be relaxed into a loose position so that the next day you will be able to skate. In this chapter we will discuss the importance of warming up and cooling down, as well as provide a few specific ideas on cross-training that may help your training. Although not all injuries can be prevented, 10 to 15 minutes before and after every session will not only improve your condition and flexibility, but may save you weeks or months off due to injury.

Benefits of Warming Up

Why should we warm up before we skate? According to exercise physiologist and trainer Jessica Regnante, warming up is important because it increases the blood flow to the muscles and organs, allowing the body to work more efficiently. Cold muscles are tight and inflexible. Thus, warming up is important, as warm muscles are more pliable and less likely to be torn or injured.

Warming up is good for the body, and it prepares you psychologically for practice or competition. The human body is an orchestra of ligaments, tendons, and muscles. Just as an orchestra warms up, you must warm up too. Each day your body is a little different. You may be tired, or you may have eaten different food than you usually do, or you may have muscle stiffness in different places. You may also have outside stresses from the rest of your life. Warming up focuses you and prepares you for the work you will do in practice or competition.

Although it is often difficult to find the time for it, warming up is crucial to your development and improvement as a skater. Dr. Burdenko believes that you should plan your warm-up like you plan a performance. Wear comfortable clothes that allow you to move, and work in warm areas that will help your body to warm up; instead of stretching next to the ice, stretch in the locker room.

Know the sequence of how you will warm up. Begin by breathing to increase the oxygen and energy in your body. Then move into a general warm-up working the whole body from the upper body down. You should start with an active motion moving the upper and lower extremities, moving without pain. As you begin to stretch, begin with non-weightbearing activities, in different starting positions, moving from horizontal to sitting to standing. Last, move into dynamic stretches, moving the body as you stretch. Then work specific areas. If you have a sore area, begin away from that area, gradually working toward it. For example, if you have a sore shoulder, begin working from the lower body up so that the body will be warm before you gently approach the sore area. Play with the intensity of your warm-up and stretches, beginning easily and then increasing.

Keep in mind that without preparation, stretching sore muscles is dangerous. Begin by stretching and warming up the whole body, moving on to sore areas at the end of your warm-up. Regnante breaks her warm-up into three parts: she has skaters begin with a general whole-body warm-up to increase blood flow, followed by sport-specific flexibility exercises, and then specific warm-ups such as jumps or lifts.

As you work, focus your mind and body. You shouldn't stretch while you are trying to do other things. Doing so is careless and can be dangerous. Focus on stretching your muscles and know what you are trying to accomplish. Tendons and ligaments cannot stretch; only muscles can stretch. You should be completely in tune with your body to monitor how it is responding to the activity. Imagine what you are trying to accomplish and picture your muscles and body achieving the desired results.

General Warm-Up

Skaters should begin with a general warm-up. The purpose of the general warm-up is to increase blood flow to the muscles to get your body moving. The warm-up should not be very long, maybe 5 to 10 minutes. A 15-minute warm-up would be ideal. However, as skaters are often rushed for time, just make sure your warm-up involves all of the major muscle groups in the body and raises your body temperature enough to cause light sweating.

An example of the general warm-up would be jumping rope, bench stepping, or, if available, the slideboard. Jump ropes are inexpensive, easy to carry, and can be used anywhere, so jumping rope is a great general warm-up. Almost all rinks have stairs to practice bench stepping. Practice stepping up with your right leg and letting your left leg meet it, and then step down with your right leg, followed by your left. Then practice stepping up with your left first. The important thing is to maintain a consistent rhythm: up, up, down, down. As you are first working on this exercise, you may wish to stabilize your arms by placing them on your waist. If the movement is easy, move your arms in opposition as if you were running.

The slideboard is also an effective general warmup, as it is the most skating specific. If your rink does not have one or you have never seen them, a slideboard is a curved piece of Plexiglas that allows skaters to practice stroking on the land, but with motion. As with bench stepping, it is important to maintain a steady rhythm as you warm up on the slideboard so that you will raise your heart rate.

A light, 10-minute jog is also a good way to keep the blood going. If you jog, keep in mind that you need to jog for skating. I used to run, but I had to stop for a while because I hurt my Achilles tendons. I liked to sprint and go fast to feel the same freedom and speed I feel when I skate. However, sprinting doesn't help you in skating because on the ice our skates allow us to flow, whereas when we sprint we constantly have to push to keep moving. When I ran, I used long strides to run fast, which stretched my Achilles. I later learned that I can jog, but I have to keep my Achilles tendon short, using a quick up-and-down, almost bouncy jog. In addition, the right kind of shoes are very important.

Sport-Specific Flexibility

Once you are warm, you are ready to stretch. Two types of stretches are *static* and *dynamic*. Most skaters begin with static stretches and advance to dynamic stretches. It is best to move to dynamic stretches only after establishing a basic level of flexibility. These stretches take the joints through their full range of motion and prepare you more adequately for skating. According to Dr. Burdenko, dynamic stretches are good for two reasons: first, because life is dynamic, and second, because they warm you up much faster than static stretches. In addition, dynamic stretches help to improve your balance. Whether you are sitting or lying down, you are moving when you do them and you are taking the joint and your body through its range of motion as you work to stay on balance. The movement improves your coordination. It is a much more thorough and effective method of stretching.

The important thing to remember about dynamic stretches is that they should not be jerky. They should have a smooth and consistent flow. Always start in a conservative, small range of motion and gradually increase it.

You will always use your abdominal muscles when doing these stretches so that you will be very controlled. You should also focus on maintaining strong posture alignment and pelvic stability in your stretches. In any sport, athletes focus on strong posture alignment. The strong positions you create through alignment on the ice give your skating style.

As you work on stretching, know what part in your body you are stretching. Muscles stretch, but ligaments and tendons do not. In addition, in most stretches, we work to increase the range of motion. There is a difference between elasticity and flexibility in muscles. Dr. Burdenko describes flexibility as joy in your performance. It also includes your ability to change. Elasticity has to do with the quality of your muscles, as well as your ability to recover.

In any stretch, it is very important to continue to breathe. Many skaters hold their breath as they are stretching. This only keeps them tense and tight, thus working against the stretch. Breathing encourages your muscles to stretch. As you begin a stretch, inhale. Then move into the stretched position. Stay in the stretch for several deep breaths. On each exhalation you will relax a little further into the stretch. Another way to think about it is that each exhalation should be twice the amount of time as your inhalation.

Dr. Burdenko taught me to combine stretching with shaking. As he says in *Overcoming Paralysis*, "During the warm-up phase of exercise, shaking increases the temperature in the tissue and loosens tight muscles and joints" (page 48). He also advises that you shake during and after exercise as well, starting to slowly shake your arms and legs and progressing faster. Visualizing what muscle you want to stretch is also very important. Doing so will help you to focus and will increase the benefits of the activity.

Though each skater has different strong and weak muscles, a few muscle groups are commonly tight in figure skaters' bodies. These are the quadriceps (front of the thigh), hamstrings (back of the thigh), adductors (inner thigh), hip/gluteal region, and the calf/Achilles tendon. As you stretch, you should prioritize by working on your tighter muscles first. One tight muscle might not allow another muscle to stretch, so it is important to start with the tighter muscles and then move into your more flexible muscle groups.

Specific Warm-Up

Once you have warmed your muscles and made them flexible, you are ready to move into the warm-ups that directly relate to the work you do on the ice—perhaps practicing your jumps or lifts. Jessica Regnante quite often turns the skaters over to their coaches at this point or allows them to work alone to complete the remainder of the off-ice warm-up. The specific warm-up will vary depending on what you need to do and should be designed with your coach. If you are practicing your jumps, it may take only a few minutes. However, pairs and dancers should definitely warm up all of their lifts off the ice before taking them on the ice. Synchronized skating teams often practice their routines off the ice and may have specific practices that take place completely off the ice. Primarily, you should use this time to do what feels comfortable to warm up your body for your specific on-ice moves. Continue your warm-up on the ice, focusing on warming up your body for your workout.

Cross-Training Ideas

Although off-ice training often takes place in a gym, you can use a variety of other ways to exercise to augment your training in any location. Often, when I'm home watching a movie, I'm thinking, *I could be exercising*. We can do so many things in our everyday lives that help us to be more athletic and physically fit. At an airport, I always take the stairs or walk instead of taking the moving walkway. If I'm shopping, I try to park farther away from the mall. When you are in training you have so little time to yourself, but if you take the time to exercise or stretch while you are doing something relaxing such as watching TV, you will find that it feels so good that you will want to continue. In that way, exercise will become a natural part of your off-ice life.

Just as you vary your stretches so that each muscle group will be worked and none overdeveloped, you should vary your cross-training program. To be a good competitor, you must have endurance. Jumping rope, using the slideboard, and bench stepping are the best ways to train endurance, but you can also run or ride an exercise bike. These movements are the least like skating and do not offer a balanced exercise routine because they train only the lower-body muscles. However, you must establish a program that works for you, and these are other available options. In training for endurance, you will work for 25 to 30 minutes. The important thing is to keep the movement steady. You need to get your heart rate up and keep it going for a longer length of time than a general warm-up.

While these types of movements will build your overall condition, you may also wish to work off the ice building your artistry by taking dance classes. Dance teaches alignment, increases flexibility and range in your muscles and joints, and provides another style of movement. Dance also teaches you how to move to different types of music in creative ways. By calling some local dance studios, you can begin to take group classes. Once you settle into a style, you may want to take private lessons, asking the instructor to work specifically on moves that will relate to skating. However, a group class will allow you to try out that style without a commitment. When I was younger, many judges told me that I was not very graceful. I began to take tap and jazz to help improve my footwork. I also took ballet. I wanted to be known as a well-rounded skater who was able to really skate to her music with clean positions. Ballet has helped me to learn about stretch, coordination, posture alignment, and balance.

Ballroom dance is especially good for ice dancers, but all skaters may enjoy it. Like ballet, ballroom dance teaches greater movement through alignment. Most styles of dance were initially done on the floor, and each dance has a vast and varied lineage. Ballroom will teach you how to move to many styles of music, as foxtrots, tangos, quicksteps, rumbas, and cha-chas are all ballroom dances. It will also teach you musicality, rhythm, and how to dance with a partner.

Almost any additional movement that you do off the ice is good for you so long as you employ proper technique and do not put your body in jeopardy to do it. Some skaters, such as Elvis Stojko, enjoy karate. Others prefer to in-line skate, whereas still others like to pursue basketball or track and field. The key is to work smart and do everything in moderation. The day before a test or competition, don't run for hours or play basketball or do any other sport that might wear you out. If your goal is to become a champion skater, you need to think of your body first and take precautions to keep it healthy and in good shape.

Cool-Down

Stretching after your workout is almost more important than before it because you have just used your muscles and you are tight. I have always wanted to keep my muscles long and thin, so in stretching them out after a workout, I keep them lean and less bumpy. Also, releasing your muscles after a workout will keep you more flexible for the next time you work out or skate. If you can stretch in the water or have a massage, that is also helpful.

Dr. Burdenko has also taught me another method to release tension after a workout or between exercises. He has taught me to rapidly shake my muscles. As he says, shaking is one of the most powerful tools any athlete can use to release stress in the body. Shaking is important because after a workout your muscles are contracted and your nerves are compressed. In spending two to three minutes shaking your muscles, you will ease the contraction in the muscles and compression on the nerves, which allows for improved circulation overall and looser muscles for the next time you work out. Dr. Burdenko advises that after your practices you shake the major muscles that feel tired. For most skaters it is very important to shake the legs. However, you should also shake your arms and the other muscle groups to release tension. Make shaking a habit.

Although warming up and cooling down may seem less important than the work you do on the ice, both are extremely important to your development as a skater. In taking a few minutes before the session and a few minutes at the end, you will prevent injuries and increase your longevity in the sport. So take the time. It really will help!

22

Land and Water Exercises

In the last few chapters, we have given you all of the concepts you need for working out and developing an effective and intelligent off-ice routine. Now it's time to work out! In this chapter you will learn specific exercises that may be done on the land and in the water. Each exercise is broken into easy-to-follow steps. If performed correctly, you will not only receive a dynamic, full-body workout, but you will also work through all of the essential qualities that you learned about in chapter 20. As you work out, it's important to work safely and with proper posture alignment. If anything hurts, stop immediately and consult with a qualified professional to make sure that your form is correct.

Land Exercises

In the following exercises, we will use several different props for assistance. These include a wooden stick or metal bar, exercise tubing, an exercise belt specially designed by Dr. Burdenko, and a stability ball. We will work on exercise mats and also on a flat bench. In using each of these exercise tools, we will be able to work on all of the six essential qualities to build a balanced exercise routine. Most of these tools are relatively inexpensive and may be purchased at department stores or home fitness stores.

As you work through the following exercises, work with a professional to design a schedule that will work for you. Dr. Burdenko advises that beginners work out twice a week, intermediate-level athletes work out three times a week, and advanced athletes work out four to six times a week. You should always have one day a week off. On that day, advanced athletes should not be idle. Dr. Burdenko advises that they should be outdoors or doing other things, but they should not skate.

As you work, the goal for every exercise is to build up to 30 repetitions. You can start 2 and 2, for example—meaning 2 exercises forward and 2 backward. The next day, try to do 3 and 3, gradually increasing to 10, 20, and 30. As you work to increase the repetitions, you will also vary the speeds at which you do them. For example, at 15, you would do 5 slow, 5 medium, and 5 fast. As you build up to 30, your goal is to do 10 slow, 10 medium, and 10 fast.

Start with the major muscle groups or your weakest areas, beginning with the easier techniques first. As the exercises begin to feel more comfortable, work into some of the advanced techniques. On all exercises, think about your alignment. If possible, have a trainer work with you to make sure that you are doing them correctly. Remember that not all exercises work for everyone. These are a few general ideas to get you going, but you should develop your own program based on your specific areas of strength and weakness.

Warm-Up Walking

When you start out, Dr. Burdenko advises that you begin walking forward, backward, and sideways with different speeds, maintaining proper alignment. After a few repetitions of the movement, you may vary it by walking with an upper-body motion in different planes—three steps with your arms up, three at shoulder level, and three down.

If the pattern is the same without mistakes, you can increase the difficulty by combining walking and jogging. In this way, you do three steps walking and three steps jogging, first slow, then medium, then fast, and perform the exercise both forward and backward. The exercise may be done indoors or outdoors, depending on your preference. The main thing is to get your body moving and your heart rate up so that you will be ready to begin working out.

Stick Exercises

You may use a broomstick or a hockey stick for these exercises, but you need something long enough so that when you bend sideways from your waist one side is touching the floor. A stick is a very good tool because it is a visual that shows you when your shoulders are even and level. It is also an excellent assist in alignment and balance.

Lunge Walk

Dynamic—Obliques, upper body, and lower extremities

Essential qualities: Balance and strength

The lunge walk improves lower extremity strength and back alignment. It may be done without the stick, but using a stick allows you to work your upper body as well as your lower body. Begin with both feet together with a lifted abdomen as you hold the stick over your head with your hands at shoulder width and your arms comfortably extended. Keep your shoulders down but be careful not to lock your elbows. Take a big step forward with your left foot so that you finish in a lunge with your right leg back. Both feet should be facing forward. At the same time, bend from your waist to the left so that the end of the stick touches the ground. You will feel this stretch through

your waist and up the entire length of your right side to the shoulder. The lunge should also stretch your Achilles tendon, so keep your front foot flat on the ground and balance on the ball of your back foot. Your left knee should be over your ankle or the first few shoelaces on your left foot. Hold the stretch for a few seconds and then stand up. Repeat with the right leg forward.

Kicks

Dynamic—Upper body and lower extremities

Essential qualities: Balance, coordination, flexibility, and quickness

The kicks with the stick help to improve alignment and core body strength, vital for skaters. To begin, stand with your feet in a T position with your back leg turned out and your front leg facing forward. The stick will be at shoulder level, with your hands comfortably placed slightly wider than your shoulders. To establish a rhythm, take two steps forward; on the third step rise up on your front leg and kick your back leg into the air. At the same time, extend your elbows straight overhead so that as you kick, your toe touches the end

of the stick. The stick should be level with the floor so that you feel a stretch equally in both sides of your waist. Repeat with the other leg. The rhythm should have a constant motion so that you are evenly doing a step, step, and kick to both sides. This will also improve your coordination.

Exercise Belt

Dr. Burdenko has designed an exercise belt made of resistance tubing. The belt attaches at your waist as a normal belt does and has long pieces of resistance tubing with handles that strap around your feet and hands. The resistance may be tightened or loosened depending on what you are trying to accomplish. The resistance helps you to work through the essential qualities for a balanced workout.

Hurdles With Calf Stretch

Dynamic—Hamstrings, calf, back, and shoulders

Essential qualities: Coordination, flexibility, and endurance

This exercise will improve your coordination if done correctly. To begin, take two running steps forward. In this case, let's begin with your right foot stepping forward first. As you run, your arms and legs should be straight and will move forward and back with your hands in fists. On the third running step, kick your right foot forward and raise the opposite arm (your left). Then bend at the waist so your left arm will reach to your right toe. Your right arm should be stretched and slightly behind you. To feel the stretch in your right Achilles, calf, and hamstring, your right toe should be flexed. Your abdomen should be tight so that your spine is straight. Again, it is important to establish a rhythm for the stretch. So run evenly so that you do run, run, and stretch. Repeat starting with the left foot.

Pirouette Turn

Dynamic—Upper and lower extremities

Essential qualities: Balance, coordination, endurance, speed/quickness, and strength

This may look like a simple turn, but when you add resistance the turn becomes much harder. The pirouette turn with resistance will help build all of the essential qualities and is important for your jumps, spins, and turns on the ice. It also teaches you to control your landings, as you need to bend your knees to control your foot placement on the ground. To be-

gin, your arms will be stretched at your sides with both feet turned out. (This is ballet fourth position.) Begin with your left foot forward, and make sure that your abdomen is tight with your shoulders down and your head lifted so that you have a strong posture using your core strength. Winding from your waist, rise up on your left foot and turn to your left. Your arms should come over your head with your shoulders down so that you have good posture in the turn. Your right leg will bend with your knee forward and slightly turned out. As you complete the turn, you will gently step forward on your right foot, practicing to control the landing. Repeat with the right foot forward to start.

Exercise Tubing

Exercise tubing adds resistance to your exercises and provides a safe and effective way to train. It is an excellent tool for stretching because it mimics your muscles, allowing you to see the stretch and what you are trying to accomplish. It often comes in different strengths and may be purchased through home gym stores or catalogs. Some companies offer it in rolls that can be cut according to the length that you desire. You may also find it with handles and without.

When you work with exercise tubing, work facing the tubing and away from it. Doing so balances your muscles because in one direction the tubing assists and in the other it resists. Don't start with a lot of pressure. As you work, gradually increase the pressure by stepping farther away to intensify your workout.

Abductor Tubing Stretch

Static—Abductors

Essential qualities: Flexibility and strength

You will need a long piece of tubing (12 to 13 feet) for this exercise that can either be tied to a door handle or other immovable object or held by a friend. The important thing is that you want to feel a stretch, but you don't want to feel pain. If you feel pain, move closer so that the resistance decreases.

Lie on your back with both feet straight up in the air. The tubing will be attached around the arch of each foot. Your feet should be flexed. Your back should be pressed into the ground so that your spine is long and straight. At the same time, your arms will be extended comfortably to your sides. Take a deep breath in. As you exhale, gently lower your right leg to the side on the ground, as close to your hand as you are able. At the same time, your left leg will lower straight down to the ground. Both legs should be turned out with both feet flexed, and both shoulders should still be on the ground with the heels flexed. Hold the stretch for 15 to 30 seconds, remembering to breathe as you relax into the stretch. Inhale and simultaneously bring your legs straight together in the air in your starting position. Then, exhale and lower the left leg to the ground to repeat the stretch on the opposite side.

Crossover Stretch With Tubing

Dynamic—Abductors, adductors, back, and shoulders

Essential qualities: Coordination and flexibility

For this stretch, lie on your belly. You may wish to roll a towel under your face to keep your chin on the mat. Your arms should be extended to the side with your palms flat to the ground. The tops of your feet should be on the ground with your thighs parallel to the ground. Inhale. As you exhale, take your right leg to your left hand. You will roll slightly onto your left hip, and your left leg will turn out, but you still want to feel your right hand pressing to the ground. You are aiming to have your right foot as close to your left hand as possible. Exhale and straighten your right leg straight behind you in the air. Lower your right leg to the ground. Repeat, starting with the left leg.

Squat With Tubing

Dynamic—Abdominal muscles, lower extremities, upper body, and back

Essential qualities: Flexibility and strength

The squat works your entire body, emphasizing your abdominal muscles and down. When done with tubing, it also works your upper body and back muscles. Begin by standing with your feet together and your arms extended in front of you at shoulder level. This time, the tubing will be around your wrists. Your abdomen and back should be lifted so that you are standing with straight posture using your core muscles. Keeping your pelvis in line with your shoulders, bend your knees. At the same time, extend your arms at your sides at shoulder level. You should have perfect body alignment as you squat, so bend deeply enough to keep your knees over your toes, but not beyond them. From this position, you may increase the difficulty by kicking one leg straight out with the free foot flexed. This variation provides a stretch for your Achilles, calf, and hamstring muscles and will help to improve your balance and coordination.

Many skaters don't do squats because they claim that the movement bothers their knees. If you are doing the movement correctly, keeping your body in strong alignment, it will not hurt your knees. It will help to improve your pelvic stability, a skill that is definitely needed on the ice.

Bench Exercises

For these exercises we will use a workout bench that may be found in most gyms. However, a bench in an ice rink or a picnic bench would work as well. A bench is an important workout tool as it allows you to do lower- and upper-body strength and flexibility exercises differently than you are able to do them on the ground. Thus you have many different variations for movement to work through the essential qualities.

Bench Pushup With Glute Stretch

Dynamic—Glutes, shoulders, lower and upper extremities

Essential qualities: Balance, coordination, flexibility, and strength

Begin by kneeling on the bench. Your body should be square to it with the hands placed on each side for support. Raise your right leg so that it is parallel to the ground. Inhale. As you exhale, bend your elbows so that you do a pushup with your arms. Your right leg will rise higher into the air. Try to keep the leg straight with a slight turnout and a pointed toe. At the same time keep your spine long

and straight. Inhale, and as you exhale, bend your right leg from the knee so that it curls back toward your left ear. Inhale again. This time, as you exhale, straighten your leg and swing it from the side back around to the other side of the bench. At the same time, sit into your heels so that your leg finishes parallel to the bench on the right side with your arms straight as you sit back. This final position should give you a nice stretch in your arms and glutes as well as your hamstrings. Repeat, beginning with your left leg in the air.

Passive and Active Hamstrings Stretch

Dynamic—Hamstrings, abductors, adductors, and back

Essential qualities: Balance, coordination, flexibility, and strength

This stretch will improve not only your balance, coordination, flexibility, and strength, but also your pelvic stability. As we know, it is very important for skaters to have strong pelvic and leg muscles for control on the ice. Begin sitting on one side of the bench so that you are perpendicular to it. Put your right leg

on the bench so that it is extended to the side. Your arms should be stretched to the side and you should be lifted out of your waist with a long back and firm abdomen. Flex your right foot so that you feel a stretch in your Achilles tendon, calves, and hamstrings. Both hips should be facing forward so that your left leg is bent and on the ground in front of you. Inhale. As you exhale, simultaneously lift your arms over your head and your left leg into the air. Your shoulders should be down with your neck long. For maximum benefit and stretch, try the position in two different ways: once with a flexed left foot, and once with a pointed left foot. Hold for 15 to 30 seconds before you release and switch sides.

Swiss Ball Exercises

The Swiss ball is also referred to as a physio ball or stability ball. The ball generally costs $20 to $30 and can be purchased at most home fitness stores. The ball exercises build core strength and balance and coordination, using all of your major muscle groups.

Kneeling on the Ball

Static—Core muscles and pelvic stability
Essential quality: Balance

Any time you work on balance, it is important to have a straight spine with good alignment. Begin by kneeling on the ball with your arms stretched to your sides. You may wish to have a friend help you by holding one arm as you work to balance. Try to balance in the middle of the ball, using your breath to relax your muscles into alignment. In this position, you may use your feet to help you stay in a solid position on the ball. This is actually cheating, and you should try to relax your feet and use your core abdominal and back muscles to keep you balanced. As a variation, try balancing with your arms overhead with your back and neck long and your shoulders down. Try to hold the position for 30 seconds. Repeat.

Shoulders on the Ball Bridge

Dynamic—Back, abdomen, pelvic stability, hamstrings, and quadriceps
Essential qualities: Balance, coordination, and strength

This exercise will contribute to your balance and coordination, but it also is

an excellent exercise for your pelvic stability and strength. Begin by putting your shoulders on the ball and making a tabletop. There should be a 90-degree angle between your ankles, knees, and hips. If this is hard, hold this exercise for 30 seconds to a minute for

2 to 3 sets, resting between. Once you can hold the position, try to increase the difficulty by rolling your body up the ball so that you finish sitting on the ball. Keep your arms at your sides and use your abdominal and back muscles to help straighten your body. Repeat.

Low-Level Jumping

Dynamic—Back, abdomen, and all lower extremities

Essential qualities: Balance, coordination, and speed/quickness

In 1994, one additional exercise that I did on the land was to jump down from a low-level bench. I began with simply jumping straight down and landing on both feet. Once my movement improved, I began to add a turn in the air. First, I jumped with a 90-degree turn in the air, working up to 180 and finally 360. Doing this taught me how to cushion my movements so that I could break down the landing portion of my jump.

Water Exercises

Although it may not be possible or even practical for you to work in the water, if you have access to water I strongly advise taking advantage of it. Most local YMCAs and many schools have pools, so it may be easier than you realize. Water workouts are extremely beneficial as water provides support, assistance, and resistance. It is also a safe and effective way to work out. As you work in the water, begin working with a flotation device such as a buoyancy vest or belt until you feel comfortable with the movements. Doing so will remove gravity and will make you less prone to injury.

You can do several simple things to get started. Just as we walked on the land, it is important to repeat the motion in the water. This time, however, you will use a buoyancy wet vest and will work in chest-high water so that your feet do not touch the bottom. The buoyancy wet vest should be adjusted so that it is comfortable. You don't want to feel that you are either sinking or too high in the water. Begin walking forward and backward, later adding side-to-side steps and crossed steps. As you do this, maintain your alignment and try to keep your abdomen, back, and pelvis strong. Pelvic stability helps you to find control and balance in your upper and lower body.

In the following exercises, we will work with several devices. These include the buoyancy vest or belt, rings, water barbells, a noodle, and a workout station or stairway. Several very simple exercises may be done with these devices to achieve maximum benefits. For most of the exercises, we will work in the deeper end of the pool. For the average person, water that is at about chest level is considered the deep end. Exercises that may be done in the shallow end will be specified. Just as in the land exercises, we will work with sets and repetitions. We will also work intelligently. Keep in mind that if something hurts, you should stop doing it until a qualified professional is able to watch and assess your technique.

Ring Exercises

For these exercises we will be use rings attached to the gym's ceiling. The rings should be attached to a rotating pulley so that you can pull them to your desired length and they are able to rotate. You will be in the deep end of the pool for these exercises. Although this may not be possible in all pools, if you are able to find a pool or rig up something similar to this, the rings can be extremely beneficial. They allow you to work your upper body using the water's assistance and resistance.

Pirouettes With Rings

Dynamic—Upper body and abdominals

Essential qualities: Flexibility, speed/quickness, and strength

This exercise develops strength and pelvic stability. It also directly relates to the work you do in jumps and spins. To begin, hold the rings with your shoulders down and your elbows slightly bent. Your body should be vertical in the water. Using your upper-body strength and abdominal muscles, bend your arms and pull yourself up to the rings while at the same time rotating in your standard spin direction. While you are spinning, the rings should be at shoulder level, with your body in its best alignment. Repeat, turning in the opposite direction.

The Rope Swim
Dynamic—Upper body, back, and abdominals
Essential qualities: Coordination, flexibility, and strength

Begin by holding the rings overhead with your elbows slightly bent. Lie in the water on your back with your knees bent. Rocking forward onto your belly as you kick your legs, swim forward so that your elbows straighten behind you as you hold the rings. Your legs will straighten behind you as you sweep them from your back to the front. At the same time, rock onto your back. Your arms will still be straight as you hold the rings, and your legs will lift out of the water into the air so that they are in a V shape. To finish, bring your legs together in the air with your toes pointed so that you are in a pike position. Bend your knees and you are ready to begin again.

Long Handbars

Water long handbars come in a variety of shapes and sizes and may be purchased at fitness stores or aquatic stores. They also come in different levels of buoyancy. This is very beneficial because, depending on the exercise needs, they may be submerged to offer several variations for one exercise.

Side Running Swim

Dynamic—Lower extremities, back, and shoulders

Essential qualities: Coordination, endurance, and speed/quickness

This exercise provides a complete body workout. Begin with your left side in the water as you hold two long handbars. Your left arm should be extended so that the left handbar is over your head, and your right arm should be extended so that the right handbar is at your thigh or hip level. As quickly as you can, begin running sideways, kicking one leg over the other so that you turn in a circle. This exercise is meant to build endurance, so it is important that you run as quickly as you can. Run for 30 seconds. Then try to run backward on the same side. Repeat, beginning with your right side in the water, running in both directions.

Handbar Spiral

Dynamic—Lower extremities and upper body

Essential qualities: Balance, coordination, and flexibility

For this exercise, you will use only one long handbar. To begin, submerge the handbar in the water so that your left foot is on the handbar and your chest is above water. Your back and abdomen should be lifted so that you have strong alignment, and your arms should be extended to your sides at shoulder level. Bend your left knee and keep the middle of your foot on the handbar, but don't hook your toes around it. Extend your right leg behind you. Inhale. As you exhale, straighten your leg so that you are in a low spiral position. Bend your knee to return to the starting position. After several repetitions, switch legs so that you begin with your right leg on the handbar and repeat the exercise.

Noodle Exercises

For these exercises we will use a noodle. These are very easy to find, as they are in many department, fitness, and aquatic specialty stores. Many children may play with noodles in the summertime, but they are also effective tools for working out in the pool. Like the water handbars, they are buoyant, yet may be submerged for exercise variations.

Noodle Sit

Dynamic—Abdominals

Essential qualities: Balance, coordination, and strength

The noodle sit provides a fun and different way to work on your abdominal muscles. Begin by lying on your back in the water. Extend both arms and legs and place the noodle under your knees. Using your abdominal muscles, pull your body forward to a sitting position. Your arms should be extended to your sides at shoulder level the entire time. Repeat the exercise with different speeds, varying how quickly you move into sitting position. Gradually increase the number of repetitions.

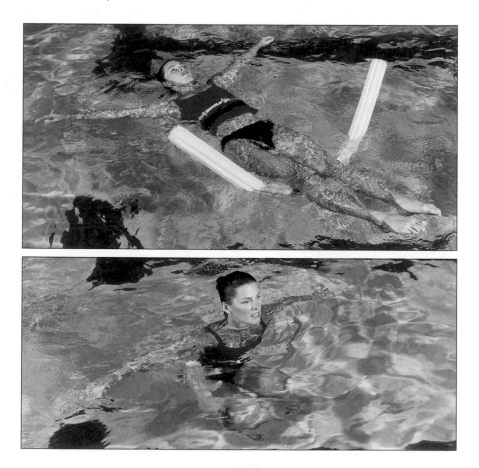

Workout Station

For the next exercise, we will be using a water workout station. Many pools have a stairway in the deep end, which provides similar benefits to the water workout station. In using the workout station or the stairway, you can work your upper body in a variety of ways to improve your strength. The additional benefit of working in the pool is that it is both fun and less stressful on your muscles.

Sit to Stand

Dynamic—Hamstrings and upper body

Essential quality: Strength

This exercise may seem very simple and is similar to getting in and out of the pool. However, with a slight variation, keeping your arms and legs straight, you are able to work your muscles in a different way. To begin, sit in the water with your feet on the bottom step and your arms on the handlebars. Both your arms and legs should be straight. Inhale. As you exhale, stand up so that your arms are bent and you are standing on the last step. From about your thighs down, you will be submerged in the water. Your upper body should be lifted, with your abdomen tucked in and your back long for good alignment. Bend to sit down. Repeat.

Shallow End Dancing

The water may also be used to help you work on the artistic and technical skills you need on the ice. Of course, if you make a mistake in the water you don't have to worry about getting hurt, so practicing jumps or lifts in the water is an extremely safe way to work on your skating skills. Just before the Olympics, Dr. Burdenko asked me to bring in my music for my program. In the shallow end of the pool, he had me perform my program. The water added resistance, but it was also very relaxing.

In working both on the land and in the water, you will have a multifaceted training program that will keep your workouts intense, interesting, and fun. As you work out, always work carefully and with intelligence. Remember, you only get one body in life and you want to work in ways that will not only decrease injury, but will also increase your ability to become a better skater.

Part 6

Preparing for Competition

What is it that separates a skater who wins the Olympics from one at the same level who can't make it to the national championships? Is it musical selection? Costume? The way programs are put together? Or is it something a bit harder to pinpoint—that certain "it" quality? Throughout this book I have discussed skills and techniques to improve your skating. In this section we will talk about some things that many skaters think of as "intangibles." These are music, choreography, costumes, and putting everything together to compete. These things may seem hard to define, yet you can develop certain processes and skills related to them.

As we move into the next section, remember that this is the fun part that combines all of your skills. You will work to be mentally, physically, and artistically strong to create the total skating package. As we discussed in part 5, it is not only how you prepare on the ice but also how you prepare off the ice that can help you to improve. One area that we have not previously mentioned is nutrition. Proper nutrition is crucial to your development as an athlete and can determine your mental and physical preparedness for the day. It's good to start your day eating something hot in the morning; I'm a big fan of oatmeal because it is filling and helps to stimulate metabolism.

It is also beneficial to eat five or six times throughout the day. This does not mean that you will necessarily eat more, but you should eat small meals at regular intervals. I've found that when I've done that I've felt my physical best. In that way, I was not stopping and restarting the digestive process and my metabolism. I was always keeping it active, and, in the process, was always burning calories. It also helps your body to feel more consistent because you are never fighting through the action or reaction of extreme hunger.

Finally, it is very important that you drink enough fluids. By the time you realize that you are thirsty, you are already dehydrated. This makes your muscles tired and can make you sluggish. In addition, for adults, alcohol does not help. Red wine takes the oxygen out of your blood. I always notice if I'm on tours and I've had a glass of red wine the night before, my thighs are exhausted by the end of my program from the lactic acid buildup. So you must make sure that you not only get enough fluids but that they also are the right fluids for skating.

Another aspect that we have not discussed involves the day-to-day process of working. In learning to become a better skater, it is crucial that you have fun. You need to keep your workouts interesting so that you will enjoy the process. Each day that you skate, set manageable goals for your improvement. If you are having an off day, think about what is going wrong so that you can be better prepared the next time. You also should occasionally give yourself permission to have a bad day. Maybe you didn't sleep well, or there was traffic on the way to the rink that day that made you late. If you set a daily goal and work to complete it, you will build a positive trend to your sessions. Each time you skate, you should set one or two goals for the day, such as "Today I will skate with my head up" or "Today I will work to spring higher on my Axel so that I will be able to work on my double tomorrow." I've seen Brian Boitano and his coach work on his programs without any jumps or spins. For that day, he will work on his head to make it more effective so that he is not only interpreting the music with his feet, upper body, arms, and legs, but with his head as well. It is a fun way to make your practices more interesting. These skills will help you to establish a goal and work toward it so that on days when you are tired you can focus to use your ice time in the best way possible.

In addition to setting daily goals, you also need to set yearly goals. These goals should be attainable, but give you something a peg or two above your current level to work toward. For example, you may wish to work on making your jumps more consistent that year, or you may want to pass a certain test or qualify for a specific competition. In setting a yearly goal, you will keep each day in perspective as it relates to your whole experience. Focus on your skating each day that you are at the rink. Think about what you are doing and where you are, not what you did and where you were in your practices. Doing so will allow you to continue to enjoy what originally drew you to skating and will keep your practices fun!

23

Music

Good music is one of the most important aspects of any skater's presentation in competition or shows. Over the years I have been very lucky to work with many good choreographers and coaches who have helped me to choose my music. Paul Wylie and I used to joke that our coach Mary was gone for the whole spring looking for music. It was an exaggeration, but after every season she was off looking for music and editing it. I still trust her to help me edit and cut my music because she not only knows what the judges look for and understands what works for skating, but she also knows me. We once selected a piece of music with a five-minute drum section for my competitive program. Mary wanted as many dings and crashes of the drums as she could get so that the music would be effective for my footwork section. She very carefully edited the music, making 20 cuts to get 20 different crashes of the drums that we later emphasized when we began to work on the choreography.

Music is very powerful. The music that you select to skate to can completely change your image and look. For a skater, music is a partner, producing emotion and movement. We are always looking for a piece that makes us want to skate. In this chapter you will learn about finding, selecting, and editing music for skating.

Musical Goals

Music fills our everyday lives to the point that we often don't recognize it. Whether it's the soft drone from a passing car's stereo, the themes of television shows or commercials, or, of course, the radio, music surrounds us. For skaters, the everyday music of our lives can translate into a wonderful piece for the ice.

When searching for music, think about what you are trying to accomplish or portray with your routine. Although you have many ways to go about narrowing your never-ending search for good music, two usual paths are taken. Skaters either pick a theme or an emotion to portray and then select the music, or they hear one piece of music that they love and then build a routine around it. As you look, be sure to consult the USFSA Rulebook to see whether any rules dictate the music for your level.

It is also a good idea to have someone help you in your search. Mary usually chose my music because she knew my skating, was experienced with skating and music in general, and listened to so much music that she had a ready-made library of possibilities. I could spend $300 on new music and not find one piece that I wanted to skate to. However, if I'm looking for music for someone else it seems much easier. I still call Mary and say, "Do you have anything for me?" Occasionally she doesn't, but usually she will have heard something that isn't quite right for anyone else but would be great for me.

In some cases you may have a separate person who choreographs your routines. If you are working with a new coach or choreographer, tell him or her what you might want to do so that he or she has somewhere to start. The choreographer should also have seen you skate so that he or she can help to pick music that will fit your body type and your style. I think it is worth the money to have someone help you in this way even if they are not in skating. You may turn to a dancer or a musician to help you in this process.

You and your coach or choreographer must also agree on or find a way to compromise on the type of music that you will be skating to. It should be something that you like, but if you are collaborating with another person to create the routine, you also want them to feel comfortable with what they are creating. If they don't like the music, they may not put in the effort that you will expect, and the process will be much more difficult than necessary. Keep in mind that you will hear your music daily for several months. You may even choose to keep it for two seasons. Therefore, it has to be something that you like and something with enough depth to challenge you over a long period.

Selecting Music

Once you have chosen three to four pieces that you like, bring them to the rink. Your music will sound entirely different booming out of the loud-

Music sets the mood for the program's choreography.

speaker than it did in your car or at home. Skate to it and have people off the ice listen to it, because it may sound OK beneath the speaker but sound harsh in the corners or off the ice.

In some cases you may be able to skate to vocals, but be careful that they do not overpower you. If a piece of music is stronger than your skating, it will make you look slow or might not fit your personality. It's more difficult to pick a good piece with vocals than one without them. It's hard to edit them so that they are not too long and so that you have the highs and lows and emotions you want in the skating. Some songs feel very emotional, but when you try to skate to them you realize that the melody is too repetitive. In addition, many songs with vocals fade at the end. It is very important to have a strong ending because you need something that both lets the audience and judges know that it is over and leaves them with a very positive impact at the end. I often have endings added by music editors or musicians. However, it can be difficult to get access to that service, so it is best to find a piece with a strong ending.

I skated to music by Queen two years ago. It was a very emotional and powerful piece and would have been appropriate only in certain settings. A young skater would not have looked right skating to it because it would not have been appropriate for his or her age. If the music is too fast or too powerful and you cannot skate fast enough, it will actually make you look slow. The music should fit not only your skill level but also your age. If it is too cutesy or too sexy, it will not look right.

Skaters have long chosen two combinations of music: the fast–slow–fast, or the slow–fast–slow. These are relatively accepted, but there is a push to try new combinations. Jane Torvill and Christopher Dean broke new ground with their 1984 Olympic gold-medal–winning performance to Ravel's *Bolero.* That piece is one long crescendo. Modern skaters have returned to the idea of choosing one piece with variable tempos rather than several pieces. In some cases this can be beautiful, but it can also be boring. Music should have a change in tempo and skaters should have fire behind their movements. If they look the same throughout, they may appear to be sluggish. Music should have variations to not only make it interesting but also to show the skater's versatility.

If you select more than one piece of music, keep in mind that they should flow together. It doesn't have to sound continuous if you may want a dramatic stop and tempo change, but all the pieces should fit. Whether they continue a theme or rhythm or are of the same era, they need to blend into each other so that a jarring inconsistency doesn't distract from your skating. Depending on the transitions or the kind of choreographic statement you're making, the pieces may need to be in the same mood and key.

Finally, in selecting your music, don't expect it to do everything. You can't express every emotion you have ever felt in four minutes and do your technical elements. Your routines should focus on one or two themes. That's why we pick different music from year to year: to show the different sides of our personality and our depth.

Once you've made your choices, dance off the ice, skate, interpret, and visualize skating to it. If it's something that gets your blood going and you can see and feel it visually, it's a good piece. If it sounds good in an arena and you feel excited about working on it and feel that it will help you to accomplish your goals technically and artistically, it's right for you.

Editing

Mark Militano (1973 U.S. pairs champ with his sister Melissa) wrote both of my short programs for both Olympics I competed in. They had to be 2 minutes and 40 seconds, and they started at about 7 minutes long. Mark wrote the music and kept cutting and editing it to get all of the proper crescendos so that the music would have the most impact. Having properly edited music is important to your program. You may have beautiful music, but if it is not properly cut it will lose its effect.

Now that you've made your selections and know that you can make them fit together, you and your coach should make hard cuts. These cuts will be rough to show where you think the music should be split. With today's advanced technology, you may be able to make fairly good cuts, but you will still want to consult a music-editing specialist. Use a stopwatch to time exactly how long each piece will be and at what point you would like it cut within your overall routine. For example, if the second piece is 45 seconds long and should start 1 minute and 45 seconds into your routine, you'd write this: Piece 2, 45 seconds, 1:45 in routine. Write any additional notes, such as how you would like the transitions smoothed, and take it to a professional.

Professional music editors can change the recorded volume and cut music to the note. It is best if this is someone who understands both skating and music and has high-quality equipment. If you do not have a skating music editor in your area, you may wish to speak to a local radio station. They may have greater access to available music editors and can make recommendations.

Although edited music may not sound that different from what you are used to, you will always notice the lack of polish in recordings with bad cuts or poor sound quality. Bad edits can sound like blades on cement. If the two pieces of music do not flow together, such as a slow section into a fast section, you may need to edit in a dramatic start and stop between the two pieces. It's also really important to listen to all of the instruments in the pieces and the melodies to make sure that you are not making it uncomfortable for people to listen to. And you really don't want to hear the click of the tape in the music. When I first started, I had a record. They later physically cut the music on a tape and taped it back together. Now, it's all on computers. You can stretch pieces out or tighten them so that the music will flow properly. You should not hear the music and see the skater separately. The edits of the music should flow together just as your elements flow together.

Taking Your Music on the Road

Make sure that you have copies of your music on CD and on tape. Most of the competitions do want CDs now, but there are still a few rinks that do not have CD players. A CD is good because you can put both your short and your long program on it, giving you less confusion and less to carry. It's also a good idea to keep a library of what you've done. 1984 Olympic bronze medalist and professional skater Jozef Sabovcik has a CD with about 10 different programs from the past five years. It makes it very easy for him when he travels because he only needs to bring that one CD.

Keep in mind that you should keep extra copies of your tape or CD at home. A skating bag is not the place to keep all versions of your music. They can get lost or broken, and tapes can stretch with temperature changes. Have several copies made, and keep only one in your bag. The additional copies should all be made by the professional, not tapes that you make at home, because those will be lower quality. When you compete, take at least two originals with you, giving one to your parent or coach for safekeeping. Make sure that they are clearly labeled with your name, level, short or long program designation, and total playing time. You may also need to know the exact titles of the songs and the composers or singers. Also, put your phone number on the tape in case you forget it at the competition. But don't forget it!

When you are not at the rink, occasionally listen to your music. Once it is choreographed, you will be visualizing your routines. Listening to it away from the rink also helps you to pick up subtleties and really hear it before you skate to it.

Finally, you may think that the process is over, but it's never finished. You will always be in search of the elusive song or piece of music. You can't possibly have heard all that there is to hear. One day, when you least expect it, you could hear the music that will help make you a champion!

24

Choreography

I wasn't allowed to compete or have a program with music until I could consistently land my Axel. I really wanted to skate to music, so I worked very hard to get my Axel. It took a while, but when I finally got it, I was so excited. I got my first music, from *A Chorus Line,* and I competed in the Boston Open a month before I turned 10. I didn't have great spins or a lot of style at the time; I just went fast and jumped as much as I could. As I got older, I realized that it is important to be a well-rounded skater with variety in presentation. A big part of that, as we talked about in chapter 23, is having good music. Another integral part is having strong and interesting choreography to go along with your music. Up to this point, we have expanded your knowledge of how to do specific skating moves individually. However, competitions would be boring if every skater did a spin or a jump without any sort of connecting steps between them.

In the beginning, great skaters were only considered athletes. Now we use the term *artistry* to describe a skater's program or style. Just as writers work to expand their vocabulary, skaters must expand their vocabulary of movement. In this chapter you will learn principles of choreography, how to build a wide base of movement, and specific choreographic tips and finishing touches like expression. The hardest part of choreography is breaking out of a comfortable style. Remember that you will never find out what you are capable of if you do not allow yourself to try.

Expression and variety are important elements of choreography.

Choreography Goals

Your life story and experience have a direct effect on how you skate. A skater who has been classically trained in ballet will bring that knowledge and style of movement to the ice, whereas a skater who has been trained in folk dance will have that style of movement on ice. In chapter 22, we discussed dance as a cross-training idea and noted that it can be anything from ballet to hula to ballroom dance. The important thing is to expose yourself to as many different styles of movement as possible. This may include taking classes or simply attending many different types of performances, such as dance, music, and theater. Notice how the various performers handle themselves and the audience.

In this process, you will need to consult a choreographer. My coach Mary not only helped me pick my music but also helped me choreograph my programs. In the beginning she would set the choreography for me and teach it to me. Later, our work became more of a collaboration as we set the jump placements and the layout together. If it was anything fast, I did the dance moves and she would tell me what she liked.

For those who don't work with a coaching team, it's a good idea to bring in an outside voice with fresh ideas as your choreographer. Many skaters don't try a choreographer because they are afraid of offending their coaches. It's important for the coach and the student to be honest with each other in recognizing their talents. Ultimately, the coach–student relationship will be strengthened because each will have been truthful with the other in working toward the best overall presentation for the skater.

Look for a choreographer whose programs have a distinctive look with each skater. Quite often skaters from a certain coach or training center have a "homogenous look," according to professional choreographer Collin Sullivan. He adds, "As a choreographer, you have to tailor and custom match the music and movements to the person who's going to perform them." Therefore, you need someone who is creative, who understands your needs as a skater, and who is not afraid to try new styles of movement.

Occasionally you may also wish to branch out from your regular choreographer. Trying someone new will allow you to experiment with a different style, increasing your versatility. Over the years I have worked with dancers and people outside of skating. I have worked with Russell Clarke for many of the numbers in ice theater shows because he is wonderful with detailed moves, which are more visible in the close setting. When I was young I worked with a ballet coach, Kathy Collins, and she would come to the rink and watch me skate my programs. Even if you don't hire a new choreographer, bringing in an outside consultant to look at your work is a good idea.

Creating the Program

When you are first taking your music onto the ice, both you and your choreographer should play and interpret. Pay attention to what you naturally feel in the music and use each other to help you remember what you did. Some choreographers prefer to diagram a routine on a sheet of paper and then take it to the ice. In the case of a synchronized team, the choreographer may need to create in this way to keep all of the skaters organized. In the case of dancers, pairs, or free skaters, the skater and choreographer often get their best ideas when they are just playing.

As you do this, also keep in mind what big moves, such as jumps or lifts, you plan to incorporate. For me, we knew that the triple–triple was tiring and took a lot of energy, so we would try to do that early in the program. For the triple Salchow, I needed a calm time in the music, so we often put it in the slow section. We could almost hear in the music where the jumps should be placed not only to accent the music but also where they would work best for me. As you think of the jumps or other elements you would like to include, keep in mind that you should be able to perform the jump 80 percent of the time in practice. If you aren't able to perform it with that success rate, you really can't depend on it in competition. When an audience is watching, things that usually come very easily are much harder, so you need the confidence of knowing that you are able to perform it consistently in practice. Otherwise, the whole program will become about that one move, and you will never settle into the performance.

Sullivan recommends working from the feet up when you are starting. In this process, you will naturally see where the edge takes you and where you want to direct it. Work on including the body, with arms and expression, last. While music does dictate movement, in starting with expression, you've worked on the finishing touches before you've set your base of movement.

The arms are a bit more interchangeable. Once, when I had planned a number for a show, I was asked to change the music at the last minute. Within a day, I had to find music and rechoreograph the program to fit the new music. I took moves that I had done in previous routines, and by changing the arms and adding a few new moves, I was able to prepare a new program. It's mostly the attitude that goes into your elements that distinguishes them. Whether it's soft and elegant or sharp with energy from the arms and your upper body, the look can be completely changed to make the movement look fresh.

Look at your choreography in terms of the different shapes that you are trying to create. In order to create truly interesting pieces, you need to have a variety of level and shape changes. Also pay attention to the shapes and patterns that you draw on the ice. Mary and I used to try to come up with different patterns. For one program, we made a triangle in one footwork section. Of course, now skaters are required to do diagonal, straight-line, or circular footwork sequences (see the USFSA Rulebook for specific rules for your level). However, it is also a good idea in other sections to think about how the program looks on the ice so that you are not always skating in the same directions or always forward or backward. Many times I drew my programs on graph paper so that I could see how they looked. The process has actually turned into an artistic endeavor as I now create artwork with drawings of my programs on them. It is also helpful because you see what patterns you leave behind with your blades.

Pay attention to how the routine covers the ice. A good program reaches all corners of the rink and is not skated up and down the middle or the sides.

Many skaters do their major elements in the same place. Try to vary where your major moves occur and be creative in the placement of your jumps. Lutzes don't always have to be placed deep in the corners. Obviously, the setup for any jump, lift, or spin should be comfortable. However, you should also try new ways to enter and exit your elements to give your choreography originality.

Connecting Moves With Music

We often hear people say that skaters need to skate to their music. This idea has many possibilities. You can skate to the beat or to the melody of your music. If there are vocals, you can also skate to the phrasing or make your movements coincide with certain words. This doesn't always mean that in a slow section you have to skate slowly or that a fast section requires fast movements. In a slow section, you should still be skating powerfully, but your movements may be more elegant or soft. You can play with the music by double timing a slow section or skating halftime to a fast section. Many rinks work on this in power skating classes by having skaters skate to different pieces of music to teach themselves how to skate to the beat or the melody. When Paul Wylie taught power classes, he used to bring a drum and bang it so that the skaters would only skate when the drum told them to move. It was a good way to teach skaters how to listen to and respond to the tempo of the music.

The important thing is to feel that you are in control of the music, not the other way around. You can actually command the music by borrowing a few beats to hold an extension and then moving quickly out of it to stay on top of the tempo. In addition, pay attention to the highlights in your music. This may sound obvious, but you will see many skaters completely ignore the fact that their music is building to a climax and do a slow spin or a crossover. The music dictates how you will move and what you will do. Listen to it, paying attention to its accents and musical flourishes. Then work on its subtleties and smaller accents so that you will fully use your music in interesting and creative ways.

Finishing Touches

Overall, your choreography should be challenging but comfortable. Sometimes, once you get used to the choreography, you realize that something is not working, or you are consistently late for a part or early for a part. As you do a program more and more, it can feel as if it spreads out. Keep in mind that the choreography is not set in stone and can be changed to fit your needs.

As you work to set the choreography, think about the finishing touches, such as toe point, stretching your arms and legs, the placement of your head,

Effective connection of moves with music is a mark of a well-choreographed program.

and your posture. My ballet instructor used to tape popsicle sticks to my hands. I had a habit of skating with them curled up like a ball and they were too weak and not attractive. At the time it drove me crazy, but now I really appreciate it. I am very tuned in to other skaters who do not finish their lines, and one of my biggest pet peeves is people who skate with their thumbs out so that their hands are in an "L." If you think of putting your thumb on your palm, you can avoid this. For me it is like a stretched line with a flexed foot. If you can't point your toe, turn it out so that it looks pointed. At the same time, continue to work on pointing it so that the line will always appear finished. Many skaters forget that their eyes are a vital ingredient in performance. When you take a speech class, you are told to look at each person in the room as if you were speaking only to him. Obviously, if you are skating in a big arena, you can't look at every single person, but you should look at the audience. It is a positive way to bring them into your performance.

Expression is the hardest part of performance and is very difficult to teach. For some skaters it comes very naturally. For others it is a skill that is constantly being refined. Expression is something that can be drawn out of skaters, but you must be willing to do things that may feel a bit silly at times. It is best if you can find the motivation to create the expression naturally. However, you may also be able to think of specific things to do if the expression is not coming naturally. Professional ballroom dancer and former international competitor Mark Nocera has taught expression to a wide variety of ballroom dancers of all ages and levels. If his students are not able to express on their own or feel silly, he helps them to build a repertoire of facial and body movements to work from. To that end, he gives his students concrete expression tips such as, "scrunch your forehead" or "drop your eyes" to coincide with their movements. This helps them to build a repertoire of movements and determine what they feel the most comfortable doing so that the expression will become a part of them. In this way, skaters and dancers can express using definite imagery. Of course, as you do this, you want it to feel and look natural, not forced or insincere.

Actors are always trying to figure out their motivation for acting a certain way. Even if you feel that you haven't experienced enough to emote to the music, keep in mind that you have other experiences that apply. Children's emotions are much simpler because they haven't had as many relationships, but they have had experiences that made them happy or made them sad or angry. You may need to remind them that for an exciting part in the music, they should think about riding a roller coaster. Or, for a sad part of the music, you can remind them of a time that they fell and hurt themselves. As a coach, it is very important to remind children that they have had these experiences and to relate to them on their level.

Do your programs in front of the mirror, with and without the music. It is the clearest and fastest way to assure that you feel good about how you look. It is also an excellent way to check on pointed toes and stretched positions. In addition, it allows you to see what facial and body movements look good on you physically with and without the music. Remember that a good performer touches the audience and pulls them into the performance.

In all, your choreography should expand your skills as a performer and showcase your athletic talents. Keep working to broaden your vocabulary of movement, your expression, and your technique on ice. In the end, you could become the ultimate skater, combining wonderful technique with an artist's interpretation and style.

25

Costumes

You have already picked your music and begun to work on your choreography. Now it's time to figure out what you will wear to augment your music and choreography. Just as it is important to have variations with your music and choreography, the same applies to your costuming, makeup, and hair. In this chapter we will talk about matching costumes to your music, assuring a proper design and fit, and putting the finishing touches on a costume. Although you may think that costumes are not important, a poorly chosen costume reflects on your overall package. So, as always, pay attention to the details and choose something you can be proud to wear.

Costume Goals

I have had many costumes. Some have been designed by a costume designer, and some I found on a store rack. Once I bought a dress off of a rack for $55, and I can't tell you how many compliments I got on it. It just so happened that that company's dresses fit me perfectly, and the skirt fell right on the hip where it should be. It was as if it had been made for me. For that event I wanted something very simple, as if to say, "Watch my skating, not my dress." Of course, in skating, the costume is an integral part of the package that you put together for the audience to see. A good costume can augment your skating, or it can distract from it.

Before you design your costume, you should already have selected the music. The process of finding and selecting the music often takes so much time that the costume comes at the last minute, so it is nice to begin the preparation early. The music helps to give you ideas for your costumes. The costume should not only match your music, but it should also complement your choreography. For example, we think of soft, flowy fabrics for waltzes and fiery colors with stiffer fabrics for tangos. In some cases you may need to actually do research, particularly if the music relates to a specific era or ethnicity, such as 40s swing or polkas.

You need to know what looks good on you. You may love certain styles but know that they don't work for you. Know what everyday regular clothes look good on you. Men may think that this advice applies only to women, but they also need to know what is visually pleasing on them—for example, some men can't wear pleats, and some need a wider leg cut.

Also, know which fabrics move well on the ice. In skating, people often want to use chiffon, for example. Some chiffons are stiff and don't drape, so you need to know a bit about the material. If you have someone else sewing it, he or she may prefer to select the fabric. However, some costume designers prefer that you select the material. Generally, you need something with at least two-way stretch. You should know where fabric and bead stores are in you area and which stores have the most available for the best prices.

You will also need to think about your skating and what moves you incorporate in your choreography. Your costume should be comfortable and should not prohibit your movement in any way. At the 1992 Olympics, my white dress didn't stretch enough for me to be able to get the proper windup for a triple Lutz. When you are skating, the last thing you want to think about is, *My costume is killing me!* You want to be able to think only about what you have trained for and what you need to do.

Finally, as you prepare to design your costume, don't forget to refer to the rules. Skating has so many rules, and they change constantly. There are times that you may think that a sleeveless dress or shirt would make sense with the music, but unless you are willing to risk the deduction, it is not worth it. Always consult the rulebook and make sure that you are within the guidelines. As I've said in other chapters, you need to first know the rules in order to break them.

Design and Fit

It is generally a good idea to hire a costume designer. You put a lot of money into training and preparing for a competition. A poorly designed or ill-fitting costume is distracting and ultimately conceals your hard work. You can find a designer by talking to other skaters. If you like someone's costume, ask him who made it. A good costume designer should know skating very well, and, possibly, have made skating costumes in the past. He

When designing a costume, consider details such as sheer sleeves, as on this costume worn in the1992 Olympics.

or she should be a trustworthy professional who understands how certain fabrics drape and move on the ice and knows how to make clothes fit.

On your first costume planning session, bring your music and any ideas or notes that you would like to discuss. If you've never worked with the designer, you will probably have a measuring session, so don't wear baggy clothes. Be prepared to discuss any concerns that you may have and any of your ideas about what is flattering to you. Ask the designer to draw a few ideas, with rough cost estimates, that you can show to your coach. The design should be something that you like. If you like it, you will feel fantastic wearing it and will ultimately skate better. You may have to pay the designer a deposit at this point.

If you choose nude material as part of your costume, it should match your skin color and tights as closely as possible. Men's pants shouldn't be too long or baggy, and shirts shouldn't be too loose. Some designers place dresses over a leotard; others place a skirt only over a leotard. Either way, the costume needs to fit like a glove and should show off your body in a pleasing manner that does not distract from your skating.

You or the designer can do specific things to adjust the fit. At the 1992 Olympics, I had sheer sleeves. The costume didn't have seams on the shoulders. Now I see people try to do sheer fabric on the upper body and, in certain materials, there are seams. If you can, avoid cutting up the costume. In that particular dress, the elbows got a little puckered, but the look was so perfect, and I knew that I wouldn't wear the dress that often. Another time, the zipper in a dress broke because it was very dainty. I wore the dress roughly 60 times. In some cases you have to know how the dress will be used and factor that into the design.

If you are wearing boot covers with a unitard or pants, pay attention to how the boot is placed. One of the girls in a show at the ice theater was having a unitard made. I mentioned to the designer that they should make sure not to put a seam at the end of the ankle. Instead, they put the seam only at the top of the foot and the leg was measured down to the skating boot's heel. That way, they just added the toe box and the boot covers looked less clunky.

I've also had a dress made by the Boston Ballet. They did something interesting to keep my dress in place so that it didn't move around as I skated. The part just above the trunks from the hipbones in the back wasn't actually attached. When I bent down, the trunks stayed in place. In another costume, the skirt was very heavy and we didn't want it to disturb the upper part of the dress when I jumped and spun, so we tacked it lower in the back. Sometimes, if you have a slight swayback, you also need darts in the back to keep the costume nice and slim to your body. Or, if the bottom half of the costume is very heavy, the designer may put a belt inside to keep it snug.

You may have already decided whether you'll use beads. The decoration does not have to be complicated. Many skaters actually opt out of beads, instead choosing fabrics that glisten or have sheen versus flat fabrics with lots of decoration. Whatever you decide, keep in mind that the dress is seen 90 percent of the time from a distance, so little beads or beads that are the same color as the fabric often don't show.

Make sure that any beads are affixed tightly. For my 1992 Olympics dress, the beads were somehow steamed on. I'm still not sure how they did it, but the beads will never come off. I've had costumes that had the beads glued on, and I've discovered that there are good glues and not-so-good glues. If you speak to enough people, they will be able to help you or your costume designer find good glue. If you opt to glue on beads, keep in mind that the glue should be used neatly so that it cannot be seen on the costume.

Many people opt out of gluing and sew the beads on. For certain looks, you may want to glue, and other times you may wish to sew them on. Often I use crystals that can only be glued on. They add shine, but in some cases you may not want that shine and would prefer to have the beads sewn on for a different look. Pairs, dancers, and synchronized skaters need to pay

© Rob Tringali, Jr/SportsChrome USA

Simplicity in costumes can be effective and pleasing to the eye.

special attention to the placement of beads. In the areas that you will be touched, beads have a tendency to fall off. Also, you don't want to beat up your partner's hands with beads that continually dig into them. Keep in mind the movements that you do with your partner as you design the decoration. If you have beads that are hanging, you have to be careful that neither you nor your partner will get caught in them.

Finishing Touches

When the costume is finished, always skate in it one or two times before you compete to make sure that it fits, and leave enough time for minor alterations. A good costume designer is fast, but no one can make miracles happen, so you need to give the designer time to complete the process.

Any minor alterations should be free of charge. The designer usually guarantees fit. If, however, you somehow dramatically change size or want to change the design completely, it's not the designer's responsibility to do the work gratis.

You can do some additional things to make a costume fit if you are running out of time. If the seat of the dress will not stay in place, I have used carpet tape in a pinch. I have also used body glue to keep the upper part of a costume close to my body. The glue that I like the best is called It Stays and it comes off only with water. It can be very helpful in places where you may normally use nude fabrics. In one instance, I also used it to hold a headband on my forehead. It is just another thing to make you more comfortable when you are on the ice.

Keep in mind that once you take the ice you should leave your costume alone unless you are really having a problem. So often we see a skater take the ice and begin fussing with the costume or pulling the leotard down. Do the preparation off the ice so that you do not have the problem on the ice.

Skates

Finally, keep in mind the details. Skates are an extension of the overall look, so you should have clean skates and laces. I had the dirtiest skates going when I was training. When I competed, it took me two hours the night before to polish my skates. I liked the white skate with the black heel, so I would not only polish the skates but also put clear nail polish over the black. It is a little trick that helps to keep your skates clean in performance so that the first time your skates touch, the nail polish, not the black paint, comes off. It is also important to have new laces and check your screws. I used to wear new laces when I competed. Some skaters don't like to break in new laces. However, you can easily break them in by putting your foot in the middle of the lace and pulling them before you put them on. And later, when you do put them on, you can deeply bend your knees a few times to make sure they are comfortable. People actually talked about how clean my skates were at competition, so it was worth the extra effort.

Another helpful tip is to tape the laces. Once, when I was at a competition, Dick Button called me over in a practice and asked me to tuck in my laces. I hated doing it because it really hurt. At the time, I kept them out in competition because I didn't want to be thinking about them when I performed. However, a few years later, I discovered that I could use clear packing tape over the laces so that they would not flop around as I skated.

Tights are also very important for the women. Tights should somewhat match your skin color. They won't be an exact match, but they should not be distracting. In addition, shiny tights can be very distracting. If you are wearing tights or fishnets over your skates, the tights should not cover the heel. On fishnets, it's a good idea to tape the hooks to keep the tights from ripping as easily. In the past, I have been in shows where I had to wear fishnets and I had white skates. I would cut old tights that had holes to make boot covers so that they would be the same color.

Hair and Makeup

Hair, nails, and makeup should be carefully chosen and tended to. Both men and women should wear a little makeup under the bright arena lights. Always do your makeup in bright lights, then step 15 feet back from the mirror or have a friend across the room tell you if you've done enough. You should especially make sure that your eyes and lips are visible. If you are wearing foundation, it should match your skin tone and be blended so that where you have applied the foundation and where you have not is not distinctly visible. The best tip is that you should take what you naturally have and enhance it. If you are playing a spider, you may need to do something a little different, but in most cases, you should have a somewhat natural look. It might be a good idea to consult a makeup technician if you need ideas. A big part of the process is knowing what looks good on you and making sure that the makeup complements you as well as your music, choreography, and costume.

Your hair should be neatly pulled back and sprayed so that it won't look messy as you skate. You can do so many interesting things with your hair that you should try new things. If you have long hair and you plan to wear a ponytail or a bun, the placement should follow your jaw line in most cases so that it finishes the line. If you are doing a Spanish number, you may want it a little lower. If you are trying something that requires bobby pins, make sure that the pins are not visible. They should be about the same color as your hair and you should criss-cross them. I knew someone who tripped on a bobby pin and ruined her knee and can no longer perform, so it is important that the pins be secure in your hair and hidden. In addition, keep in mind that simple pieces in your hair are the most effective. You don't want your hairpieces to be distracting. Long hair that is not pulled back or trundles along your face are not ideal for competition. The hair can fly into your face and get stuck in your eyelashes, or it may be frizzy. In most cases, you want your hair to be neat. Always try out your hairstyle before you compete or perform. That will give you confidence that your hair will not be distracting.

Remember that costumes, skates, hair, and makeup are all a part of your overall presentation and showmanship. Try to look the best you can because others will see the sense of professionalism you bring to all aspects of your work and will admire you for it.

26

The Total Package

Throughout this book I have talked about paying attention to the details in your skating. The music, choreography, and costumes are some of the details that give you a complete look on the ice. If you listen to enough professional athletes, you will hear them say that they are constantly working on the elements that most people think they have already mastered. The reason is that they never believe that they have finished. In this chapter we will discuss how all of the details come together to make the "total package." We will also look at ways to overcome performance anxiety and learn specific things that skaters can do to mentally prepare for a competition.

Presenting the Total Package

From the moment you take the ice at a competition, you are being watched. Judges look to see that you have prepared adequately in terms of your costuming, posture, and presentation. As you begin to stroke to your starting place, you reveal how powerfully you stroke and your skating confidence. You also begin to reveal some of those details that we have repeatedly mentioned: Do you have pointed toes? Do you have stretched extensions? Is your head held high? As you take your opening pose and the music begins to play, you reveal your sense of style and expression. During the routine, you reveal your technical and athletic skills, musicality, and the strength of your choreography. If you skate well, you reveal the level of

Aim for good extension and limb position at the beginning of a program.

preparedness you have set to get to this point. As your program nears its end and you begin to feel tired, you reveal your on-ice and off-ice conditioning. And, as the last notes are played and the music comes to an end, you reveal your ability to stay focused and keep your mind on each element as it occurs.

Each moment that you are on the ice in competition, you reveal how much time and effort you have put in to ensure your success. This carries positive and negative aspects because all the preparedness in the world does not necessarily guarantee you the medal you deserve. However, in working on each attribute of your program, you are giving yourself the best chance to become a complete skater. If you remember to polish your boots and pay attention to how you look on the ice, you will feel more confident. If you spend some time each day warming up, stretching, and working off the ice, you will become stronger. If you work on making each step build speed, you will have to work less to gain momentum. Although these are all relatively simple ideas, each one is a puzzle piece. In placing the pieces together, you will create the picture that sets you apart.

Learning to Compete

In 1993 I was competing at the world championships. It was the year after I received the bronze medal at the Olympics, and many people thought that it was my turn to take the top of the podium. Everything seemed to be going great. My practices were going well, and after the short program I was in first place. I felt great, except for one thing. I had an ingrown toenail on my big toe, my vaulting toe, which was so bad that the doctors decided to remove it between my short and long program. The next day, I fell to fifth. The pain was excruciating, but I didn't want to use it as an excuse. I felt that if I could have kept my head together, I could have been OK. The problem was that I didn't know how to compete. It sounds strange, I know, but learning to compete is a skill that needs to be developed, just like landing a jump. In that competition, I skated last for the long program. I waited 35 to 40 minutes from the time I finished my 6-minute warm-up to the time I competed. What are you supposed to do during that time? At that point, I had no idea, but through practice I learned.

Practicing Competition

Until that point I thought that practicing my program was practicing for competition, but through sports psychology lessons I soon learned that preparing to skate at a competition involves very specific work and skills. After that competition, I began to practice competing about three days a week. One day I would pretend that I skated first. I'd do a 6-minute warm-up and skate my program first. Two days later, I'd pretend that I skated fourth. I figured that I had about 22 minutes, so I had to figure out what I needed to do. I realized that if I just sat and waited, my muscles got cold and I would get nervous. Sitting did not allow me to get my nervous energy out. Of course, for everyone this is different, but I needed to stay active. I was always somewhat nervous that if I did too much exercise before I skated, I would be tired when I got on the ice. I realized that didn't make sense because we practice more than four minutes a day. In my daily practice sessions, I was doing double and sometimes triple run-throughs of my program. I skated multiple sessions in a day. Therefore, a good warm-up was not going to make me too tired.

At the end of my program, I used to feel my legs tighten. I always felt that if I could just stop the music for 30 seconds and stretch my quads, I would be fine. I realized that the tightness in my legs was from nervous energy, so if I could really warm up, I could get rid of that feeling. I would sprint for three or four laps down a hall or wherever I could at the competition. My arms and legs would feel tight at the end, but that was when I knew that I was just starting to get loose.

Proper Training

As I became more intense about learning to compete, I also started improving my daily run-throughs. I used to call my long program "the four-minute death march." Evy and Mary strongly enforced double run-throughs. I worried so much about how I would do those double run-throughs that I would skip an element in both routines. I realized that was kind of silly, and if I could do all of the elements without skipping, it actually made me less tired because I stopped worrying and, as a result, increased my confidence. Preparing for a competition is really about proper training. You need to know before you compete that you are able to do all of the elements in your program 80 percent of the time.

At the competition, I realized that there is nothing wrong with taking my skates off after my 6-minute warm-up. Many skaters think that they shouldn't take their skates off because they worry that they won't tie them the same way the next time. We tie our skates several times a day when we are training, so it doesn't make sense to worry about not tying them correctly. The trick is to make sure that you leave a whole program before you to put your skates back on and to make sure that they feel OK. That gives you time to do the exercises or things that you need to do before you skate.

Knowing What Works for You

Some skaters like to listen to their music before they skate. I always found that sitting and concentrating on my music made me tighter and more anxious, so I needed to listen to something else and not focus totally on the competition to stay relaxed. I actually used to listen to comedy before I skated. At the Olympics, I remember Evy turned to me and asked what I was listening to. I was listening to a tape about two guys who would make prank jokes. It was very funny. I let Evy listen to it and he was crying because he was laughing so hard. Just as Dr. Burdenko reminds his athletes, when you smile, you relax about 250 muscles, so in keeping your mood light and happy, you often stay loose and have a better performance. However, do keep in mind that you need to figure out what will work for you. If it's not working, try another way and keep working on it until you figure out what you need to do before you skate.

Finally, make sure that you not only prepare how you will handle your off-ice time at a competition, but also think about what you need to do when you take the ice for your warm-up. I always started out with my stroke-around, then a waltz jump and a single Axel. I found that the first stroke around the rink and the waltz jump were more tiring than my whole program because my adrenaline was so high. After 15 years of skating, I'm still doing that warm-up. From there, I usually went into doubles and occasionally triples. I would mostly do a few jumps and a few spins between taking a sip of water. I often didn't do the last minute if I skated first or second. I mainly needed to feel the ice and skate around to wind down. That worked for me, but you and your coach need to plan what you will do so that you won't be on the ice worrying about it.

Preparing for a Competition

In preparation for competition, keep in mind that you prepare to compete or perform all year. As you get closer to the competition day, you want to do the same things that you've been doing all year. The only difference is that as you get closer to the actual competition day, you want to make your workouts a little less strenuous. You should not be learning anything new, just keeping up what you already have. Primarily, you want to keep up what you have been doing so that your muscle memory is intact, and try to stay loose and in tone, not tight and tense.

The Power of Optimism

The hardest aspect for most skaters in creating their total package is controlling their minds. Some people call it having a "winning attitude," whereas others call it optimism. Building optimism is a daily task, like building strength or creating more centered spins. Before the '94 Olympics, I realized that so much was happening that I needed my coach to be very positive. We had always sort of teased each other, and he would say things like, "That's pretty good, for a girl," which, of course, just got me fired up and ready to prove him wrong. However, at that point, I realized that we needed to stop that. I felt so ready mentally, but I needed to physically prepare and I didn't want anything negative to take away from my preparation. From that point on, we worked that way and I was so grateful that we did it together and that he was willing to do that for me.

Goal Setting

You and your coach must set a goal for the competition that is entirely unrelated to results, and you need to be realistic in what you hope to accomplish. For example, maybe at this competition you want to work on skating with more expression and better presentation than you did at the last competition. Or maybe you want to work on skating with greater speed or edge depth or try to land all of your jumps. Keep in mind, though, that if you have been missing a jump every day in practice, that is your performance level. So if you miss one thing in a program you shouldn't get mad at yourself. Competition and performance are very nerve-wracking. We try to feel that everything is the same, but when you are in a new building with an audience and judges watching, you have extra pressures. Don't add to that by putting too much pressure on yourself. If you do miss an element, you have to forget it. In thinking about the last thing that you missed, you will forget to think about the skills that you need to remember for the next element, and you may miss it. Work to stay calm and try to work on one element at a time. Whatever the overall competition goal is, work toward something that you can control versus something that you can't, such as results. It will ultimately make you a better competitor who uses a winning attitude to skate your best.

In the end, remember that if you do not perform to your expectations, it is OK to feel bad about it, but don't beat yourself up. At the same time, if you have success, it is OK to feel good about it. When I was competing as an

© Rob Tringali, Jr/SportsChrome USA

Confidence and competitive spirit—both qualities that make up the total package.

eligible skater, I was taught not to show emotion about how I felt about my successes or shortcomings at competition. It got to the point that when I won a big competition, I could barely admit that I was excited and proud that all of my hard work had paid off. I knew that I had skated well, and the other skaters had also skated well, but I had built a wall around myself and I didn't want to appear as if I was bragging. You may have times when you win and you are not satisfied with your performance. It's OK to feel that you can do better and to express it. Of course, I'm not recommending that you throw your flowers or cry when the marks are announced, but you shouldn't be afraid to express your emotions in a healthy way. A champion skater knows that the results are just the scores on the wall at the end of the day. The true results come in how you feel about your skating and how you performed.

Keep in mind that presenting the total package is really about trying to make yourself as strong physically, mentally, and artistically as you can be. As you work to take your skating to the next level, remember to have fun in the process. It is, after all, the process of learning how to be better skaters that makes us continually fall in love with the sport and want to work hard to be our best.

Summary

As you move through your career in skating, remember that skating teaches you about yourself—about your own body and what you are capable of. It gives you knowledge that you can use anywhere. When I began skating, there was not an "afterlife." If you were lucky, you could maybe tour for a few years or teach. Skaters used to think that once their competitive careers were over, they were finished with skating. But now so many new opportunities exist beyond coaching or skating professionally. If you think that you want to be a professional skater, you have many opportunities within the field. However, if you are finished with that aspect of the sport but still want to be involved, other possibilities abound. Shows need lighting designers, set designers, music technicians, and costume designers. In addition, there are opportunities within television and within the promotion and marketing of skaters. You can also teach, or even write a book! If you love the sport, the opportunities are limitless.

Good Luck and Keep Skating!

References and Suggested Reading

Berman, Alice. 1998. *Skater's Edge Sourcebook: Ice Skating Resource Guide*. 2nd ed. Kensington: Skater's Edge.

Boeckl, Wilhelm R. 1937. *Willy Boeckl on Figure Skating*. NY: Moore Press, Inc.

Burdenko, Igor N., and Julian A. Miller. 2001. *Defying Gravity: The Burdenko Method*. Igor Publications.

Burdenko, Igor N., and Scott Biehler. 1999. *Overcoming Paralysis*. NY: Avery.

Burdenko, Igor N., and Edmund Connors. 1998. *The Ultimate Power of Resistance*. 2nd ed. Wayland: The Burdenko Water and Sports Therapy Institute.

Fassi, Carlo. 1980. *Figure Skating with Carlo Fassi*. NY: Charles Scribner's Sons.

Ford, Bernard. 1996. Footwork. *Skater's Edge* (March/April/May): 1-11.

Grant, Gail. 1982. *Technical Manual and Dictionary of Classical Ballet*. Revised 3rd ed. NY: Dover Publications, Inc.

Grossman, Lori. 1999. Designing woman. *Skating* (November): 20-22.

Hagen, Patricia, and Indiana/World Skating Academy. 1995. *Figure Skating: Sharpen Your Skills*. Indiana: Masters Press.

Kerrigan, Nancy, and Steve Woodward. 1996. *Nancy Kerrigan: In My Own Words*. NY: Hyperion.

Künzle-Watson, Karin, and Stephen J. DeArmond. 1996. *Ice Skating: Steps to Success*. Champaign: Human Kinetics.

Leamy, Elizabeth. 1998. Music matters. *Skating* (February): 33-37.

Petkevich, John Misha. 1989. *Sports Illustrated Figure Skating: Championship Techniques*. NY: Sports Illustrated Winner's Circle Books.

Owen, Maribel Vinson. 1960. *The Fun of Figure Skating: A Primer of the Art-Sport*. London: Arthur Baker Limited.

Shulman, Carole. 2002. *The Complete Book of Figure Skating*. Champaign: Human Kinetics.

Skubovious, Lisa. 2000. Music for skating. *Skater's Edge* (March/April): 1-11.

Skubovious, Lisa. 2000. Editing music for skating. *Skater's Edge* (Summer): 1-9.

The 2002 Official USFSA Rulebook. 2001. Colorado Springs: The United States Figure Skating Association.

Whedon, Julia. 1988. *The Fine Art of Figure Skating*. NY: Harry N. Abrams, Inc.

About the Authors

Nancy Kerrigan won her first medal at the Boston Open when she was 10 years old. Since then she has participated in more than 40 U.S. and international competitions, finishing first in 12 of them. Kerrigan is a two-time Olympic medalist, winning the bronze in 1992 and the silver in 1994. In 2000, she placed third in the ladies artistic program in the Goodwill Games. Currently, Nancy Kerrigan skates with the Tom Collins Champions and has appeared in *Grease on Ice* and *Footloose on Ice.* She resides with her husband and son in Lynnfield, Massachusetts.

© International Figure Skating/Patrick O'Connor

Mary Spencer is a professional figure skater and writer. She has taught ice dancing, expression, and freestyle to skaters of all ages and levels. As a journalist, she has written articles for *American Skating World* and *Blades on Ice* and is the managing editor of *6.0 Skate Magazine*. Mary Spencer resides in Melrose, Massachusetts.

Photo by Lynn Wayne

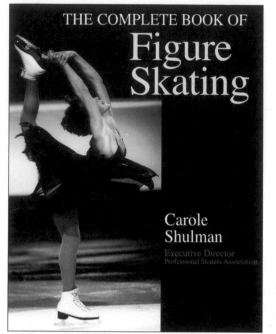